Editor-in-Chief: Barrie Pitt
Editor: David Mason
Art Director: Sarah Kingham
Picture Editor: Robert Hunt
Designer: David A Evans
Cover: Denis Piper
Special Drawings: John Batchelor
Photographic Research: Benedict Shephard
Cartographer: Richard Natkiel

Photographs for this book were especially selected from the following Archives: from left to right pages 7 Keystone;
8 National Archives; 9 US Army; 10 US Army; 11 National Archives/US Marines; 13 National Archives; 14 National
Archives; 15 US Signal Corps; 16-17 US Signal Corps; 18 US Signal Corps; 19 US Signal Corps; 20 US Signal Corps; 21
National Archives; 22 United Press/US Signal Corps; 22 US Signal Corps; 24 US Signal Corps; 25 US Army; 26 US Army;
27 US Signal Corps; 28-29 US Signal Corps; 28 US Signal Corps; 31 US Army; 32 US Signal Corps/US Military Academy
Archives; 34 US Signal Corps; 35 National Archives; 36 US Signal Corps; 38 Keystone; 39 United Press; 40 US Signal Corps;
41 US Signal Corps; 41 National Archives; 42 United Press; 43 US Signal Corps; 44 National Archives; 46 United Press; 47
National Archives; 49 US Army; 51-52 US Army; 53 World Wide Photo; 55 US Army; 58-59 Keystone; 60-62 US Army; 66 US
Army; 68 US Army; 68 US Navy; 68 IWM; 69 US Army; 69 Keystone; 71 US Army; 74 US Navy; 76 Keystone/US Navy; 77 US
Navy; 78 United Press; 79 Keystone; 80 US Navy; 81-82 Keystone; 83 US Army; 86 US Army; 86 Keystone; 87-91 Keystone; 93
Ass. Press; 94 US Army/IWM; 95 AWM; 96 US Navy; 97 US Army; 98 US Navy; 99 US Navy; 100 USAF; 101 IWM; 104 Keystone;
105-107 US Army; 108 IWM; 111 IWM; 112-113 US Navy; 114 USAF; 115 IWM; 116 US Marine Corp; 117 US Navy; 118-119 US
Army; 120-122 US Army; 123 IWM; 124 US Marine; 125 IWM; 126 US Marine Corps; 129 IWM; 130-137 US Navy; 138 Keystone;
139 US Navy; 140-141 US Army; 142 IWM; 145 US Army/Keystone; 146 US Navy; 148 USAF; 149 Keystone; 150 US Army; 151 US
Navy; 152 US Army/US Marine; 153 IWM; 154 US Marine; 156 IWM/Keystone; 157 US Army; 158-159 US Army; Front Cover
US Army; Back Cover US Army.

Copyright © 1971 by S L Mayer

ISBN 0-345-27900-X

Manufactured in the United States of America

First Edition: April 1971
Third Printing: November 1978

Contents

Impressions

The only time I ever saw MacArthur was in 1951. I was living in Evanston, Illinois and MacArthur had just been relieved of his command in Korea. The night before he had given a speech to the ecstatic cheers of over 100,000 people in Soldiers' Field, a Greek revival-style football stadium on Chicago's lakefront, after receiving the cheers of perhaps a million Chicagoans in his triumphal parade down the main streets of the city's Loop. Evanston is a rather largish, increasingly commerical suburb just to the north of Chicago, and Mac-Arthur was planning to give a short speech at Fountain Square, the hub of the small city, before proceeding northwards to what promised to be another enthusiastic welcome for him in Milwaukee. And what a welcome we would give him! Evanston and my father were arch-Republican, and knowing what a great reception the General would receive in the heartland of Senator Joe McCarthy (our hero), it seemed that everyone was determined to show up on the streets lining his 'route of victory' to greet him.

The night before MacArthur came to Evanston my father and I had a conference to plan our strategy. He did most of the planning; I was thirteen years old. Since a big crowd was sure to gather in Fountain Square, it would be no use to go there. But his entourage would come into Evanston from Chicago on Sheridan Road, close to Lake Michigan. If we stood a few blocks past the point where he came into town we might have a chance to catch a glimpse of the great man. Armed with American flags, like everyone else, we got up at 6.30 in the morning to go down to Sheridan Road to wait for his coming. Hours went by and there were many false alarms. 'He's coming'; 'no he's not'; 'oh yeah he is.' And so on. But then he came.

New York welcomes MacArthur after his dismissal by Truman in 1951

Left: With Mrs MacArthur after the
Soldiers' Field rally, Chicago, 1951
Above: Truman greets MacArthur , 1950

Preceded by several motorcycles and
police cars, there, suddenly, was
MacArthur! Everyone cheered and
waved his flag at the open car. Mac-
Arthur, seated stiffly in the back,
rose in the limousine just before
he passed where we were standing.
He turned to the crowd – it seemed
as if he turned to me – and saluted.
My father and I wept. What a man!
How could Truman get rid of him?
Why, that little pipsqueak! We'll
get rid of Truman. Why, he shouldn't
be President at all. What a terrific
President MacArthur would make!

Well, it turned out that MacArthur
felt the same way. It turned out
that Truman wasn't such a bad President after all. And it turned out
that MacArthur seemed to be in
favor of abolishing social security
and risking war against Russia by
advocating the bombing of strategic
targets north of the Yalu River,
the border between North Korea
and Communist China. But we got
a General as President, all right.
The less-colorful General Eisenhower.
MacArthur's presidential campaign
never really got off the ground in
1952 after all the cheering stopped.
'Old soldiers never die; they just
fade away', MacArthur reminded the
Congress and the Nation when he
returned from Japan to Washington.
And MacArthur faded away.

Before he died Kennedy invited him
to the White House, and he was supposed to have said, 'I should have lived
here'. President Johnson treated him

9

well too and invited him back. And
then there was his farewell address
to the cadets at West Point – his
last speech – when he said good-bye
to the 'corps'. Scratches on our minds.
And yet, although the melodramatic
MacArthur, the political MacArthur,
the man who might have been the
President, dominate one's memory
of him today, I doubt if future gene-
rations will think of MacArthur
that way. Certainly his conduct of
the Second World War in the Pacific,
and probably his reconstruction of
postwar Japan, where he received
the power and veneration due to a
latter-day Shogun, which he was,
were his greatest achievements. The
Inchon Invasion during the Korean
War was a postscript to his military
exploits – a repeat performance of
his numerous victories in the Pacific;
another successful landing, another
encircling maneuver another beachhead won. There are few today who
think that Truman's sacking of
MacArthur was unjustified. He had

to obey the orders of the Commander-
in-Chief; he refused to, so he was
fired.

We were cheering the last hours
of a great general that day on the
streets of Evanston, but people of
my generation are not always entirely
aware of the military exploits which
were the basis of his real great-
ness. He was always a political
amateur, always playing politics and
playing them badly. But he was a
professional soldier. It was there
that he was successful; it was on
the battlefield or in military planning
sessions that he felt at home. It
would be worthwhile, then, to turn
to his origins; his boyhood; his education; his military training, to
discover what it was that made Mac-
Arthur the superb military strat-
egist and the supreme egotist that
he became: the long road from West
Point to his triumphal return to the
Philippines and his installation as
postwar generalissimo of a defeated
Japan.

Left: Back in the US for the first time in 14 years, MacArthur addresses Congress, 19th April 1951. *Above and below:* In 1969, West Point honors its former Superintendent. MacArthur's words on the wall of the gym

UPON THE FIELDS OF FRIENDLY STRIFE,
ARE SOWN THE SEEDS
THAT, UPON OTHER FIELDS, ON OTHER DAYS,
WILL BEAR THE FRUITS OF VICTORY.

The young warrior

Douglas MacArthur's boyhood ideal was his father, not unlike most boys. But in Douglas's case he had a lot to live up to. Arthur MacArthur's life as a soldier covered almost a half-century of American military history, beginning with the Civil War, through the Indian wars, and up to and including the Spanish-American War. Arthur MacArthur was fifteen when the Civil War broke out, and he was recommended to Abraham Lincoln for entry into the United States Military Academy at West Point. Since all vacancies had been filled, Arthur obtained a commission in the 24th Wisconsin Volunteers, one of the most illustrious units ever to fight for the Union. General Sheridan gave him special commendation at the Battles of Perryville and Murfreesboro, and after having contracted typhoid which kept him out of action for a time, he returned to his regiment to fight under Sheridan at Missionary Ridge, putting the Confederates of

General Bragg to rout. The regiment voted MacArthur the rank of major on the spot and he was given command soon afterwards.

He was nineteen years old. Wounded on two occasions thereafter, and subsequently voted the Congressional Medal of Honor, the highest decoration any American soldier can win, Colonel MacArthur was demobilized at the end of the war, but obtained a commission in the regular army, planned to be reduced to a puny 54,000, in 1866.

This small army fought the Indians in various campaigns, and Arthur MacArthur served in many of them in the seven years he fought on the western frontier. Posted to New Orleans in 1875, he met and married Mary Pinckney Hardy, a girl descended from an old Virginia family, and whose brothers fought for the Confederacy. The couple had three children: Arthur, born in 1876;

At West Point, Class of 1903

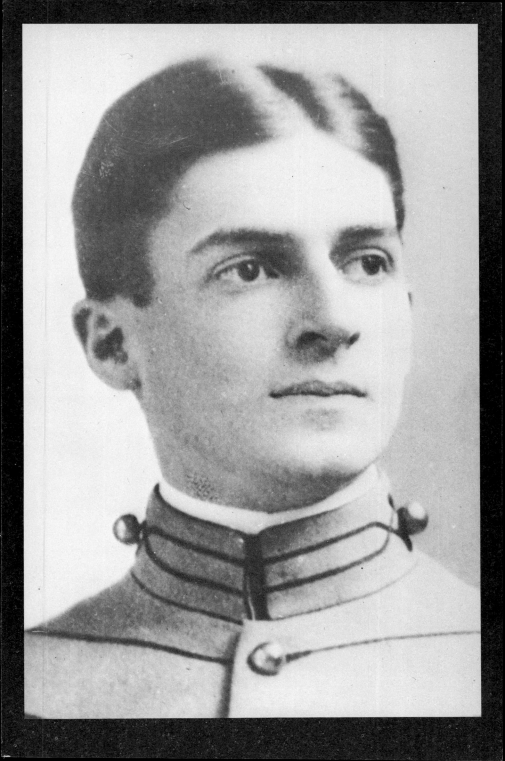

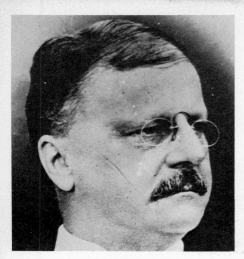

Left: Douglas (left) and Malcolm MacArthur in 1884. Douglas was then two. *Above:* Arthur MacArthur

Malcolm, born in 1878, who died as a child; and Douglas, who was born at the Arsenal Barracks in Little Rock, Arkansas, on 26th January 1880. When Douglas was four the family moved to an army base near the Mexican border, and there he was taught to ride and shoot even before he could read or write, as MacArthur relates in his *Reminiscences*. He recalled that his mother taught him his first principles, among them . . . 'a sense of obligation. We were to do what was right no matter what the personal sacrifice might be. Our country was always to come first.'

Douglas was educated in various places throughout the 1880s and '90s, wherever his father was assigned. By 1897 Colonel MacArthur was transferred to St Paul, Minnesota, and it was decided that Douglas should study for a competitive examination to be held in May 1898 for a vacancy at West Point, nominated by a Congressman from Milwaukee. He came first in the exams and went to the Point in June 1899.

By that time the Spanish-American War had broken out and had been won, in spite of the fact that the American Army had dwindled to less than 25,000, while the Spanish army in Cuba alone had many times that number. Congress voted for a wartime increase in the army's strength, and several ill-organised landings were made on Cuba. At the same time Commodore Dewey's naval forces had won an overwhelming victory over the Spanish at Manila Bay. Soon after this victory three brigades landed to occupy the capital of the Philippines and its environs, one of them led by Brigadier-General Arthur MacArthur. The long involvement of the United States and the MacArthur family in Philippine history had begun.

In the mopping-up operations against the Philippine nationalist leader, Aguinaldo, which were far more considerable than the American effort to 'liberate' the Filipinos from Spanish rule, Arthur MacArthur played a vigorous role. By the end of 1899, after Douglas had entered West Point, there were over fifty thousand Americans in the field against the Philippine nationalists, and Arthur MacArthur was one of the most important leaders of the American attack. By June 1900 Arthur MacArthur had succeeded General Otis as commander of the American contingent and as governor-general of the Philippines, and by now even more stringent measures were taken against the insurrectionists. Aguinaldo himself was captured and brought to Manila, to the astonishment and chagrin of his colleagues, and furthermore he had taken an oath of allegiance to the United States.

By July the resistance on Luzon, the main island of the Philippine group, had begun to collapse, and although guerrilla warfare continued sporadically for almost a decade, the back of the resistance had been broken. Arthur MacArthur was succeeded as civil governor by William Howard Taft, later to become President of the

Light artillery in action in the Philippines

Above: **Brigadier-General Arthur MacArthur (second from left) with his staff, Manila, 1899.** *Right:* **MacArthur in the Ardennes, 1918**

United States and subsequently Chief Justice, the only American ever to have served in the two highest offices of his country. General Adna R Chafee succeeded MacArthur as commander of the troops, and Arthur MacArthur returned to take an appointment at home.

By this time Douglas MacArthur had spent a year at the Point. By the standards of the day, which were by no means lax, discipline at the Point was very strict. Winston Churchill, on his way to visit Cuba to observe Spanish operations against the native insurgents just before the outbreak of the Spanish-American War, stopped by West Point and reported in a letter to his brother that the cadets had far less liberty than any private school boy in England. The cadets were not allowed to smoke or even have any money in their possession. Cadets entered for four years between the ages of nineteen and twenty-two. Churchill felt that such rigorous discipline would crush the individual

to such a degree that it would be difficult to make either good soldiers or citizens out of them. However harsh Churchill might have thought the United States Military Academy was, there can be no doubt that the intermittent 'hazing', or bullying, of the 'plebes' (first-year men) by senior classmates was pushed beyond anyone's definition of what military discipline ought to be.

At the turn of the century this hazing, which still goes on but which is very mild compared to what once existed, became a subject of a Congressional investigation. During his second year at the Point young Douglas MacArthur was called before the court as a principal witness in a case in which he had been an alleged victim. MacArthur was asked to name the upperclassmen involved in the incident. Overcome with a feeling of nausea, he pleaded for mercy but refused to name the offenders. He expected to be placed under arrest after he had been taken to quarters once the ordeal was over. Sixty years later he recalled waiting 'for that dread step of the adjutant coming to put me under arrest. But it never came. The names were obtained through other means . . .'

With his father gaining a certain amount of publicity for his part in the Philippine operations, MacArthur, even at this time a young man who felt the heavy weight of tradition and pride in his family's honor, worked diligently to reach the top of his class in three of the four years he spent at West Point, which included being first in the corps during his final year. He had played on the baseball team during two of those years. He was perhaps the most handsome, most photogenic cadet at the Point and was

popular with the girls, not only for those reasons, but also because he was the son of Arthur MacArthur. One biographer mentions an incident in which he was asked by a wide-eyed girl if he really were the son of General MacArthur. He replied, 'Yes'm, General MacArthur has that proud distinction'. There are no records kept at West Point for the most modest man in MacArthur's class, but it probably can be safely said that Douglas did not come first in that category.

In June 1903 MacArthur was commissioned as a second lieutenant in the engineers, at that time an élite corps of the American Army, and was sent to the Philippines, two years after his father had been sent home and who now, incidentally, was stationed on the Pacific Coast. Returning to California after a year overseas, Douglas later joined his father as an aide-de-camp in Japan

when Arthur MacArthur was sent there to report on the Russo-Japanese War. Both were subsequently instructed to make a tour of Southeast Asia and India. They travelled and talked to leading figures in Hong Kong, Singapore, the Dutch East Indies, Ceylon and India. The son remarked in his memoirs that this experience 'was without doubt the most important factor in my entire life. It was crystal clear to me that the future and, indeed, the very existence of America, were irrevocably entwined with Asia and its island outposts.' It was an opinion that MacArthur was to retain all his life.

In 1908 Douglas MacArthur graduated from the Engineer School of Application and during this period served as ADC to President Theodore Roosevelt. His father's career after the great Asian tour took a turn for the worse, however. Now a lieutenant-general, it was expected that he would be in line for an appointment as

Chief of Staff, but during Roosevelt's second administration William Howard Taft, with whom the elder MacArthur had clashed in the Philippines, was Secretary of War, and this may well have hurt his chances for advancement.

Arthur MacArthur retired in June 1909, just a few months after Taft had taken the oath of office as the successor to President Roosevelt. Three years later he fell dead while addressing the fiftieth reunion of his old Civil War regiment. He had been ill and had sent his regrets that he would be unable to attend the reunion, but the governor of Wisconsin and the two senators from that state had cancelled their engagement there as well because of the extreme heat. In this last reunion of the famous 24th Wisconsin Regiment the organisers begged their old commander to attend anyway. When the toastmaster called upon Arthur MacArthur to speak, he began by recalling the old triumphs. Then he faltered and collapsed, and the regimental surgeon rushed to his side. He turned to the audience and simply said, 'Comrades, the General is dying'. In the middle of the room the chaplain began to repeat the Lord's Prayer, and the ninety odd men came to the side of their old commander and joined in. The battle flag was wrapped around his body. Douglas MacArthur recalled that incident with reverence. Perhaps his melodramatic account of the occasion of his father's death was somewhat exaggerated; perhaps his emotional remark that 'the world changed that night; never have I been able to heal the wound in my heart' was exaggerated too. But his sense of tradition, of duty to his family and his country were exceptional. It is

enough to say that he admired his father tremendously and envied his reputation. Even at this stage in his life his chief desire was to live up to his father's name and to surpass it. But his father's lack of political subtlety, as illustrated in his alienation of Taft, was another characteristic, as well as personal courage and forthrightness, which Douglas MacArthur also was to inherit from his father.

Following his father's death MacArthur, by now a well-travelled young man with rich experiences behind him, still lacked extensive regimental and staff experience. He left his temporary posting at Fort Leavenworth in Kansas, where he met George C Marshall, who had passed the Staff College there, and went to Washington as a member of the Engineer Board. While on the Board he was able to arrange a trip to the Panama Canal Zone, where he

Above left: Already smoking a corn- cob pipe, in Texas, 1916. *Above right:* General 'Black Jack' Pershing. *Below:* Colonel Douglas MacArthur, General de Bazelaire and other officers watch manoeuvres, France, April 1918

was brought in on the last stage of the construction of the canal.

In 1911 MacArthur received some valuable experience from Leonard Wood, the Chief of Staff, by working with him on military exercises in Texas, which were meant as a show of strength to the Mexicans across the border, whose revolution was beginning to make both the Mexican landowning classes and the American government nervous. Partially as a reward for this operation, MacArthur was posted to the general staff in Washington in 1913. Only a few months after this appointment he was able to see his first active service when the United States intervened in the Mexican Revolution. MacArthur was sent by Wood to Vera Cruz to observe and report after the marines had landed there on a pretext. MacArthur had instructions that if fighting broke out between the occupying American force of over 7,000 army and marine corps personnel and the Mexican Army he was to join the staff of a field army operating out of Vera Cruz under the command of Wood himself. MacArthur distinguished himself in Mexico, and war was avoided with Mexico; MacArthur returned to Washington and in 1915 was appointed major.

America began to build up her armed forces during the so-called preparedness campaign, anticipating not only active participation in the First World War, which had broken out in Europe, but possible intervention along the Mexican frontier, where most of the United States armed forces were stationed during the more active phase of the Mexican Revolution as well as the Pancho Villa raids across into New Mexico, which General Pershing punished by invading northern Mexico with a rather large raiding party. Tension along the frontier was high, therefore, when the United States severed diplomatic relations with Germany in February, 1917.

The Zimmermann Note, which rallied Western and Southwestern American public opinion behind President Wilson, made a two-front war a very real possibility for the United States. A naval war against Germany combined with an American Expeditionary Force to France as well as a border war with the Mexicans would have hindered American military success both in Europe and in Mexico; American armed forces were simply too weak to cope. For that reason Woodrow Wilson took steps to introduce a Conscription Bill, the first attempt made in that direction since the Civil War. After war had been declared against Germany in April, a Selective Service Act had been drafted and passed through Congress. The aim of the act was to raise an army of half a million men to send to France as soon as possible as well as an additional and substantial reserve force within the United States. These early estimates, which at the time sounded high, were more than met and greatly surpassed before America's twenty-month long participation in the First World War was over. General Funston was expected to lead the American Expeditionary Force in France, but he died in February, 1917, and it was left to Douglas MacArthur to carry the news to President Wilson. In May his replacement was appointed: General John J (Black Jack) Pershing.

Pershing was described by MacArthur as 'the very epitome of what is now affectionately called the "Old Army"'. A dashing figure from West Point, Pershing fought in the Spanish-American War and later fought the Moros in the southern islands of the Philippines, where guerrilla resistance to American rule continued for almost a decade after the rest of the islands had been subdued. He had recently led the expeditionary force into Mexico; a tough character, popular among women, and thoroughly determined to prevent the AEF from being dispersed among the Allied armies once they reached France. He set up his headquarters

Snipers of the Rainbow Division in action in the Marne Salient, July 1918

in England to prepare for the hundreds of thousands of Americans who were expected to pour into Europe by the autumn, and hopefully, the spring of 1918. The Allies were sorely in need of fresh troops; millions of lives had already been lost on both sides of the Western Front and by mid-1917 the Allied cause was considerably weakened. Both Britain and France urged the Americans to come quickly.

By the end of 1917 only 175,000 Americans had arrived and only four of the twenty-four divisions Pershing promised the Allies were complete. MacArthur, who had met Pershing soon after he graduated from West Point, and who was impressed by his soldierly bearing and strength of character, was assigned to the Rainbow Division, a unit so called because it drew its members from all parts of the United States rather than from a territorial or state unit, a virtual tradition in the American armed services now, but an inno-

vation at that time. It was one of the first American units to enter the fighting in France and became one of its most illustrious divisions. MacArthur landed with the Rainbow Division at St Nazaire in October 1917, and it was soon sent to the Meuse Valley to continue its training. Both American and Allied officers recognized the fact that the American units were under-equipped and under-staffed as well as under-prepared, and it was accepted reluctantly on all sides that it would take time before any American unit was battle-ready. The Rainbow Division was one of the first to be prepared. It moved up to the Front along the Lunéville-Baccarat area in February 1918, to relieve a French unit. In his first action MacArthur distinguished himself by leading a raiding party through the barbed wire. For this action MacArthur received not only the American Silver Star but the Croix de Guerre, which General de Bazelaire pinned on his tunic and then kissed him on both cheeks. Once the Rainbow Division was ready for the attack in March, Mac-Arthur was decorated with the Distinguished Service Cross, a battle decoration second only to the Congressional Medal of Honor, when he led a raiding party into German lines. It was typical of the kind of soldier MacArthur was: courageous but also determined to create a heroic image for himself, perhaps to satisfy his own vanity, partly perhaps to live up to the reputation of his father; but certainly to impress others around him as well. MacArthur admitted as much in his memoirs. When he later received a second Distinguished Service Cross, MacArthur remarked that the citation 'more than satisfied my martial vanity'. But it would be imprudent to characterize MacArthur as merely a vain man. He was learning the art of war and was to become a master of it. He was especially impressed by defense-in-depth tactics in which the forward trenches were held by a light picket line and the main strength held back ready to surprise and destroy the enemy attack.

In July, as the Allies were being pushed back in Germany's last great offensive of the war, MacArthur was in the thick of the fighting, usually leading his men into battle, and when, on the 19th, the beleagured Rainbow Division was withdrawn after having suffered over 1500 casualties, he was awarded his second Silver Star. Once the German thrust had been halted, the Allies began a counter-offensive almost immediately, and after only five days rest, the Rainbow Division was again thrown into battle. Relieving the weary 26th Division, the 42nd (Rainbow) entered the Marne salient on 25th July and began to drive the enemy back. MacArthur compared the tactics used at this point with the tactics seen in the Indian wars in the Western United States. 'Crawling forward in twos and threes against each stubborn nest of enemy guns,' he wrote, 'we closed in with the bayonet and hand

As Brigadier-General, August 1918

grenade. It was savage and there was no quarter asked or given. It seemed to be endless. Bitterly, brutally the action seesawed back and forth'. MacArthur lived up to his heroic words. Moving inexorably forward after almost nonstop fighting for four days, MacArthur, exhausted, fell asleep. The division was again withdrawn into the reserve on 2nd August after having suffered over 5,500 casualties in its costliest battle. MacArthur was made a Commander of the Legion of Honor and given a second Croix de Guerre as well as yet another Silver Star.

By the time the Germans, themselves exhausted, with their supplies and personnel woefully depleted, had withdrawn to the Hindenburg Line, Pershing, tasting triumph, now realized his great ambition: to lead an offensive with the newly-formed First American Army aimed at the St. Mihiel salient. The main attack was to be made by the American I Corps (four divisions) and the IV Corps (three divisions, including MacArthur's 42nd.) The salient had existed since 1914 and was eighteen miles across and thirteen miles deep. Behind the front line lay a second position and across the base a third, which was part of the Hindenburg Line and consisted of wire and many concrete posts. The Germans were ready to withdraw to this seemingly impregnable line. When the infantry advanced against the line MacArthur was with the forward troops of his brigade. Within five days the salient had been eliminated and the enemy was retreating in what Pershing described as 'considerable disorder'. Almost 16,000 prisoners had been taken with 450 guns. The 42nd Division lost 1,207 men, and the First Army's casualties were about 7,000. Brigadier-General MacArthur was again awarded two more Silver Stars.

The Rainbow Division was once more withdrawn to prepare for its next offensive: the Meuse-Argonne. As veteran divisions like the 42nd

Left: Sitting in the banquet hall of a ruined chateau. *Below:* German prisoners, St Mihiel, September 1918

The fighting in the Argonne, October 1918. *Above:* A machine gun platoon advance through woods. *Below:* Tanks move up to attack

decorations as well as the Distinguished Service Medal. MacArthur's idiosyncratic methods were even the subject of a brief and fruitless investigation. For example, he failed to wear a helmet or carry a gas mask, and in fact was hospitalized after the war with a serious throat infection which, he claimed, occurred because he had taken too much gas on the front. He also had a habit of going unarmed and refusing to lead from the rear, which, although dangerous, was ultimately to his credit. When Pershing was informed of this investigation, he was reported to have replied: 'Stop all this nonsense. MacArthur is the greatest leader of troops we have, and I intend to make him a division commander'. The Armistice prevented his promotion, however, since Washington ordered that advancement of generals must cease once the Armistice came into force. Despite the heavy casualties suffered by the Rainbow Division, it achieved wide acclaim and so did MacArthur. His superior officer wrote in a letter to Pershing that MacArthur had 'actually commanded larger bodies of troops on the battleline than any officer in our army, with, in each instance, conspicuous success'. He had 'filled each day with a loyal and intelligent application to duty such as is, among officers in the field and in actual contact with battle, without parallel in our army'. There can be no doubt about the fact that, at thirty-eight years old MacArthur had proved beyond any shadow of doubt his merit as a soldier and as a leader of men, praised by his inferiors and superiors alike. No wonder some of the boys down at HQ were jealous. Despite the remarks of recent historians who have tried to revise MacArthur's grandiose opinion of himself, his First World War record leaves no doubt: he was a great soldier and deserved the high acclaim that his country and her Allies bestowed upon him.

needed rest, Pershing did not plan to use them in the first phase of the offensive, which extended over (eventually) an eighty-mile front and which was to last forty-seven days. The 42nd entered the fighting on 11th October. MacArthur organized an enveloping attack which proved successful, after which he was promoted to Major-General and awarded his second Distinguished Service Cross. Withdrawn from the fighting again, the 42nd returned to the Front on the extreme left of the American armies on 5th November, after an incident in which MacArthur, with some of his forward troops, was stopped by American troops of another Corps. Once the muddle was sorted out, both American and French forces pushed forward against the enemy in their attempt to take Sedan, but were pushed back by heavy fire. On the night of 9th-10th November, the 42nd Division was withdrawn, MacArthur was awarded his seventh Silver Star, and the next day, the Armistice ending the the war was declared.

There were those who were jealous of MacArthur's many awards, some more of which were to come his way, including a number of foreign

The warrior between the wars

MacArthur's Rainbow Division was one of the nine American divisions which took part in the occupation of the Rhineland after the Armistice. Although ill during the first months of 1919, MacArthur enjoyed the days of rest and relaxation so welcome to one who had endured so much. His admiration for the German people and their well-ordered way of life, as he later put it, as well as their thrift and geniality impressed him tremendously. He remarked that the boastful and arrogant feeling that he and the men shared towards the Germans at the end of the war was soon replaced by a 'realization of the inherent dignity and stature of the great German nation'. The well-known Kansas journalist, William Allen White, visited him in January 1919 in his house overlooking the Rhine. He was enthralled by MacArthur, and White was not one to be easily impressed, having known on personal terms almost everyone who was anyone in Washington for many years. Yet he remarked that he 'had never before met so vivid, so captivating, so magnetic a man. He was all that Barrymore and John Drew hoped to be . . . His staff adored him, his men worshipped him, and he seemed to be entirely without vanity'. But MacArthur was a great actor.

Reluctantly he left for home in April, and MacArthur enjoyed a relaxing crossing on the *Leviathan*, occupying a 5,000 dollar suite which consisted of four rooms and three baths. He regretfully remarked that although he reached New York on 25th April, 'where-oh-where was that welcome they told us of? Where was that howling mob to proclaim us monarchs of all we surveyed? Where were those bright eyes, slim ankles that had been kidding us in our dreams? Nothing – nothing like that. One little urchin asked

MacArthur in Baltimore, 1927

Above: MacArthur receives the DSM from General Pershing, Remagen, Rhineland, 1919. *Below:* As Superintendent of West Point with the Prince of Wales, 1919

us who we were and when we said – we are the famous 42nd – he asked if we had been to France. Amid a silence that hurt – with no one, not even the children to see us – we marched off the dock!'

MacArthur's welcome in Washington was somewhat warmer, if not exultant. He was summoned to the office of the Chief of Staff, Peyton C March, and told he had been appointed Superintendent of West Point. He took command there 1 June. While others who had distinguished themselves in the war were not promoted and even lost their wartime rank, like George S Patton, George C Marshall, and Joseph W Stilwell, MacArthur retained his wartime rank of brigadier-general. Furthermore, he was one of the youngest men ever to become superintendent of the Point. His immediate predecessor was seventy-one; MacArthur was thirty-nine. He had been informed that the Point was forty years behind the times, and immediately set about the task of modernizing the educational system there. Only two of the professors had university degrees; almost all the others were graduates of West Point with little or no civil education. Normally the teaching officers would stay at the Point for four years, teach as best they could without any previous formal training, and then return to a military assignment.

MacArthur recognized immediately that modern war would be fought by nations in arms, not merely small professional armies, and that these conditions would demand officers who had a broad, liberal education rather than training merely in the arts of war. MacArthur introduced a broader curriculum, brought in university lecturers to teach the cadets, and sent members of his own teaching staff to visit other colleges and universities. Many of the social abuses which members of his generation suffered at the hands of senior cadets were abolished, and

compulsory participation in team games was introduced to improve esprit de corps and to make certain that all cadets, especially ones not especially adept in athletics, would be competent to supervise games once in the service. Cadets were sent to regular army units for two months during the summer to bring them into contact with real army life in contrast with the secluded and somewhat spoiled atmosphere which West Point had created in the past. Resistance to these changes came, of course, from some members of the staff and old graduates, but MacArthur won the support of many of the officers who were closest to him, and in the end West Point had gone through the most serious reforms since the time of Sylvanus Thayer soon after the founding of the academy at the turn of the nineteenth century.

In his three years at the Point MacArthur, with the help of the National Defence Act of 1920, helped put the academy into the twentieth century. But the Army soon fell into disrepair. Demobilization and the desire of the nation to return to a peacetime basis, 'normalcy', as President Harding called it, were natural enough reactions of an America which had become disillusioned with European diplomacy after the failure of the Congress to ratify the Treaty of Versailles or to join the League of Nations. Despite the protests of Pershing, who had become Chief of Staff in 1921, the Army was reduced to 175,000 men, with only 12,000 officers, an improvement, perhaps, on the standards maintained before the First World War, but a level inconsistent with America's increased responsibilities and interests in the world outside the Western Hemisphere which came with the victory. Toward the end of his term at the Point MacArthur married Louise Cromwell Brooks, a rich divorcee. The marriage was a failure, and there was a Reno divorce in 1929.

In 1922 MacArthur was appointed to command the Manila district in the Philippines after he had made certain that the number of cadets at the Point was increased to nearly double its former size. But MacArthur was happy to be back in the Philippines after so many years, and he was delighted to see that so much had been accomplished in his absence. Local autonomous government, under the guidance of Manuel Quezon, was moving forward, and roads, hospitals, schools, docks and buildings of all sorts had appeared. General Leonard Wood, former hero of the Spanish-American War and unsuccessful Presidential candidate in 1920, had been appointed Governor-General, but Wood was a stone in the path of the Philippine desire to achieve national independence as soon as possible. MacArthur, on the other hand, was very friendly indeed with the Filipinos, and his rather outspoken opposition to those who stood in the way of the Philippine desire to achieve independence won resentment for his presence. All the same, MacArthur was given the job of drawing up a plan for the defense of the Bataan Peninsula, near Manila,

and he covered every foot of the rugged terrain there.

In 1925 he was transferred to Bal more and was detailed to be a memb of the court which was to t MacArthur's old friend, Billy Mitche who had criticized the Americ government's failure to develop h air power after the United States ha made a start on forming the nucle of an air force during the First Wor War. MacArthur considered his pr sence on the court to have been oi of the most distasteful experiences his life, and the court martial se tenced Billy Mitchell to suspensio from duty for two and a half year after which he resigned. MacArthu was subsequently accused of havir let his friend down, but MacArthu explained that he had always believe (as future events were to prove) tha a senior officer should not be silence for disagreeing with his superiors i rank and with accepted doctrine. H knew that Mitchell's paramount ir terest was in the future security o his country, but the courts martia of the type Mitchell was subjected t only require a two-thirds vote of it members to convict. MacArthur pro

bably did not vote for conviction, and he later said that Mitchell 'was wrong in the violence of his language . . . [but] that he was right in his thesis is equally true and incontrovertible'.

In 1927 MacArthur was released from his army appointment to serve as President of the American Olympic Committee, and the American team made an excellent performance at the Games held in 1928 at Amsterdam. After the Games MacArthur resumed his army appointment and was sent once more to the Philippines as commander of the Philippine Department, as the American Army command there was called. He resumed his friendship with Quezon, with whom he became extremely friendly, as well as with Henry L Stimson, former Secretary of War, now Governor-General, who was more in sympathy with both MacArthur's and the Filipinos' views on achievement independence for the archipelago. He discussed with both Quezon and Stimson the problem of Japan, which had expressed concern about the situation in China, especially after Chiang Kai-Shek had unified the

country after his successful march to the north. Japan had made a claim to having special interests in North China and for years had maintained a certain control over Manchuria through her ownership of the South Manchurian Railway and the maintenance of her troops in the area to protect the railway lines. Furthermore Japanese immigration to the Philippine island of Mindanao was on the increase, much to the consternation of Quezon and MacArthur. Although the resources at hand were pitifully inadequate, MacArthur did what he could to improve the forces defending the islands, but it became increasingly apparent that unless the island's defenses were vastly improved, the Philippines could one day be caught in a struggle for power in the Western Pacific that would inevitably involve the United States. MacArthur's warnings, in the international atmosphere which produced the Kellogg-Briand Pact, which abolished war as an instrument of national policy for virtually all the nations of the world which signed it – a treaty dubbed by cynical observers at the time as 'an international kiss' – went unheeded.

In July 1929 MacArthur was informed that President Hoover wanted to appoint him Chief of Engineers. MacArthur declined on the grounds that he lacked the engineering expertise that the job demanded and therefore would not have the confidence of the engineering profession. It was one of the wisest decisions MacArthur ever made, as Hoover subsequently offered him the post of Chief of Staff with the rank of full general to succeed General Summerall whose four-year term was to expire in November 1930. MacArthur later recalled that he shrank from the responsibility, 'and wished from the bottom of my heart to stay with troops in a field command, But my mother, who made her home in Washington, sensed what was in my mind and cabled me to accept. She said my father would be ashamed if I

showed timidity. That settled it'.

MacArthur came to the post just as the depression was making itself felt throughout the country and the world and at a point when the US Army was at its lowest point since before the Spanish-American War. It needed the dynamism of a younger, more vigorous man, which MacArthur was. He was, in fact, the youngest Chief of Staff since that office was established twenty-seven years before; and his career at West Point and in the war amply prepared him for that high office. His chief problem, however, was maintaining enough money year after year to sustain at least the basis of a modern army as well as re-equiping an army which had little more than what it possessed in 1918.

The American Army was weak, small and lumbered with obsolete equipment. In 1930, when he took command, the army only had 125,000 men and some 12,000 officers. When he left the post five years later the figures were about the same. But all this took place at a time when the annual national expenditure for the army decreased each year except for the last, 1935, when it increased fractionally. However, MacArthur managed to increase the cadet corps at West Point almost to the level that he had initially proposed for it when he was Superintendent – from 1,374 to 1,960 men. For the sake of comparison it is useful to point out that Britain's standing army was around 230,000 at this time and Russia's, 624,000. Germany, prior to Hitler's takeover, had an army limited by the Treaty of Versailles to a number in excess of what the United States maintained in the early Thirties. Small wonder, then, that MacArthur felt that for a population almost three times that of Britain and well over twice that of Germany (at that time) the United States was dangerously under-

strength and, furthermore, under-equipped to fight modern war. Nevertheless, it was difficult to focus public attention on subjects other that those which alleviated unemployment and raised the standard of living during the Depression.

It was very likely at this time, if at no time before this, that MacArthur began to fully realize the importance of public opinion in maintaining support of the armed forces. The master of the battlefield, as he feared before he took the office of Chief of Staff, would find himself in entirely different waters as a general *cum* politician. Every successful general on as high a level as MacArthur attained has, in the end, to cope with civil officials unless, of course, the state is controlled directly by the military. Such a circumstance exists in both democratic as well as authoritarian countries. In a democracy such as the United States, however, it is imperative that the generals of the army, and expecially the Chief of Staff, have close working relationships with their civilian masters. No matter what lack of expertise the soldier may think resides with the leaders of government at any given point in history, if a democracy of any sort is to be maintained, the generals must accept the fact that whether they like it or not, they are not the supreme arbiters of the state. Therefore, to achieve what they desire, they must turn to their elected masters for support. To turn to the public over the heads of their elected representatives is to court disaster. It must be said, in all fairness, that thoughts of military coup or appealing over the head of state to the people probably did not occur to MacArthur at this time, as it was to do later, but it is clear that the importance of getting along with and cajoling the President and the Secretary of the Army was necessary to improve the deplorable state the army was in when MacArthur became Chief of Staff.

MacArthur's main tasks, realizing

Left: Manchuria, 1931. Japanese troops
march unmolested through a village
Above: Unemployed riot, New York, 1930

that neither the Republican government of Herbert Hoover, nor the Democratic government of Franklin D
Roosevelt, which replaced it in 1933,
would countenance vast increases in
federal spending on the armed services
during MacArthur's term of office, were
to concentrate on improving the
equipment of the army and reorgani-
zing it. He experimented with the
development of modern tanks, which he
felt vital to the defense of the United
States, and he wanted to insure that
if another war broke out, the United
States would manufacture the most
modern military machinery rather
than obsolete types. MacArthur also
made certain that the Congress did
not cut federal appropriations to the
army by reducing its officer corps by
an additional 2,000 men. The vote in
the Congress was close – one vote in
the House of Representatives – but

the army's officer corps was not reduced. It was a shallow victory but
MacArthur won. He also made sure
that with what resources he had at
hand, he would try to develop the
nucleus of a modern air force attached
to the army, which was to be placed
directly under the Chief of Staff
rather than attached to any specific
unit. He also reorganized the army
so that four armies would be formed
which would embrace the whole of
the United States.

As Chief of Staff MacArthur made
two trips to Europe, the first in 1931.
In France he watched, at the in-
vitation of the French Government,
the annual maneuvers which included
the replacement of mounted horse
cavalry with fast, heavily armored
tanks, which impressed him and made
him even more certain that the
United States should do the same. On
his second trip to France in 1932 he
was again impressed by the degree of
mechanization that the French had
put into their armed forces, even

The Bonus Marchers in Washington, 1932. *Opposite page:* A demonstration on the steps of the Capitol. *Above:* The marchers set up camp on the Anacostia Flats nearby. Peaceful efforts to move them were unsuccessful. *Below left:* Herbert Hoover. *Below right:* Patrick J Hurley, Hoover's Secretary of War

Left: General MacArthur outside the White House, 28th July 1932. *Above:* Troops remove the marchers

during the economic slump which affected her as much as it did the United States. But then Germany was closer to France than it was to the United States. President Hindenburg of Germany openly stated that the most vulnerable targets in the next war would be the great industrial centres with their massive populations. King Alexander showed MacArthur his oxcarts which were meant to supply his Serbian divisions. Admiral Horthy of Hungary spoke of impending disaster internationally, as did Jozef Pilsudski of Poland, while he noticed that Czechoslovakia was building munitions plants feverishly. It took no military or political expert to recognize the dangers inherent in the coming of Adolf Hitler to power in 1933 and what this could mean for the future of Europe and the United States, whose histories have

been so intertwined since the founding of the American Republic. Yet Hitler was considered to be a crank by most Americans – at least at first. Japan's invasion of Manchuria in 1931 and their penetration of Inner Mongolia in 1933 were viewed as unfortunate, perhaps, but certainly not as important as licking the Depression. Despite MacArthur's warnings little could be done within the political and social framework of the times.

And the times were difficult indeed. With over a quarter of the working population unemployed by 1932, even MacArthur was forced to turn his attentions to dealing with the Depression by military means; veterans of the American Expeditionary Force, who had been promised a bonus soon after the end of the war, and who were subsequently compensated for their services in the form of insurance policies, were anxious to collect the face value of their policies as well as their long-promised bonus straightaway, without waiting for them to

43

mature. These men were out of work, some of them homeless, many of them hungry. Thousands of them marched to Washington in the summer of 1932 to demand their bonus payments, and they set up their makeshift camps on the Anacostia Flats near the Capitol. Others occupied partly demolished buildings along Pennsylvania Avenue.

MacArthur had never been a political radical. On the contrary; he looked upon the Bonus Marchers as unfortunates, to be sure, but probably infiltrated by Communists. However, initially MacArthur ordered tents and camping equipment to be sent to the Flats for the marchers and ordered out a number of rolling kitchens to help feed the multitude. This last step raised a controversy within the Congress. One Representative mentioned that if the government provided the marchers with three meals a day, hundreds of thousands of hungry Americans might make their way to Washington to join the bonus army. In this enlightened mood, the kitchens were withdrawn. In the punishing heat of a Washington summer, combined with the inaction of President Hoover, the bonus boys became increasingly disgruntled. Hoover offered to pay the marchers' bus fare home if they would only leave. Governor Franklin D Roosevelt of New York informed all New Yorkers within the ranks of the bonus army that they would be given train fare home by the state if they would only leave. But the bonus marchers wouldn't leave.

On 28th July the police began to evict the squatters living between the Capitol and the business district. There was a clash and a policeman shot and killed one marcher. MacArthur maintained later that there were few *bona fide* veterans in the group and that they were under the influence of Communist agitators. This presumption was most unlikely. There were probably a few Communists in the crowd,

Franklin Delano Roosevelt in 1932

but most of the marchers were protesting a genuine grievance, and the American public was anxious to see how the veterans of the First World War were going to be treated. MacArthur received an order from the Secretary of War, Patrick J Hurley, that the President had informed him that the civil government of the District of Columbia was unable to maintain law and order, and that MacArthur was to direct United States troops to the 'scene of disorder', to surround the area and to clear it without delay. He was also admonished to 'use all humanity consistent with the due execution of the order'. About 600 infantry and cavalry as well as a platoon of tanks were ready. Accompanied by two of his staff officers, Major Dwight D Eisenhower and Major George S Patton, MacArthur proceeded on horseback to the area where the squatters resisted. By the evening of 28th July the bonus army was driven back across the Anacostia River to their camp. Not a shot was fired and no one was seriously hurt. At 9pm the troops were ordered to clear the Anacostia Flats. By the next morning the marchers had gone, and tear gas was used to repel the marchers who were throwing rocks at the soldiers. Those who still remained in parts of the city were removed the rest of the following day. MacArthur apparently had won another victory. But a hollow one.

MacArthur insisted that it all was a Communist plot and, in fact, a few Communists were arrested; the Communist Party of the United States, apparently in a spirit of bravado, claimed responsibility for the bonus march; of course they would. Most of the American people sympathized with the marchers. In fact, most of the marchers were ordinary Americans who had felt that their government had given them a raw deal and they wanted to protest about it and to get the money they felt they deserved. MacArthur took a beating from the national press for his involvement in

45

the affair. He even sued Drew Pearson
and Robert S Allen, well-known left-
of-center newspaper columnists, for
damages amounting to $1,750,000 for
their criticisms of him, depicting
MacArthur as a pompous man-on-
horseback who had turned on his
former comrades-in-arms. He soon
realized it was a mistake and dropped
the case. Actually, there was nothing
offensive in what MacArthur did. He
merely followed orders, as the saying
goes. No one was killed, few were
seriously hurt, but the sight of the
burning camps and the sight of the
smoke from these camps slowly
drifting over and blackening the
Capitol of the United States en-
furiated millions of Americans. The
Bonus Marchers and their fate became a symbol of the inability of the
Republican government to cope with
the problems of the Depression.
MacArthur became, in the eyes of
many, a symbol of repression and
right-wing fanaticism which he was
unable to shake off throughout his

Above: CCC workers build an
amphitheatre, Arizona, 1934. *Right:* US
Army on manoeuvers, 1935

career. MacArthur may have tech-
nically done no wrong in this incident,
but he was politically naive, and was
stung deeply by the criticism he had
to endure. MacArthur was soon to
learn that it did not pay for a general
to be politically naive.

Franklin D Roosevelt succeeded
Hoover on 4th March 1933, at a time
when the country had hit rock bottom.
The new President was a very different
sort of man from Hoover, and had
promised a 'New Deal' to the American
people who were crying out for leadership. His Hundred Days of Reform
brought a new spirit of optimism to
the United States, which slowly began
to move forward again under his
leadership. One of the sweeping reforms made in these early days was to
provide money to employ some 300,000
in reforestation work throughout the
country. The army was to organize

these men into units, equip them and transport them to their places of employment, where the civil authorities would establish their camps and supervise their efforts. Civilian officials were unable to cope, however, and the army took over the entire operation with great efficiency. The CCC camps, as they were known (Civilian Conservation Corps), became one of the most popular early successes of the Roosevelt administration, and MacArthur handled the job well.

But Roosevelt's relations with MacArthur, which were to become stormier as time went on – due to the differing political philosophies of the two men as much as the fact that both were strong personalities which inevitably rubbed against each other the wrong way – began on a shaky footing when Roosevelt's new Secretary of War, George H Dern, was faced with a cut in army appro-

priations of eighty million dollars. MacArthur, aided by Dern, vigorously opposed these measures which MacArthur felt would force three to four thousand officers into retirement, discharge 12–15,000 men from the forces, eliminate field and armory drill training of the National Guard, and almost completely dismantle the technical services of the Army. MacArthur arranged with Dern to see FDR. MacArthur pointed out that the world situation was too dangerous to allow a further weakening of American defences while Germany, Italy and Japan were busy rearming. Roosevelt poured sarcasm over MacArthur's remarks, and then MacArthur's temper got the better of him. He said words to the effect that if America lost the next war he wanted the American soldier dying in the mud to spit out the name 'Roosevelt' before he died, not 'MacArthur'. Roosevelt, quite naturally, objected vehemently to

MacArthur's intemperate and melodramatic tone and shouted at him, 'You must not talk that way to the President.' MacArthur apologized and offered to resign as Chief of Staff. As he walked out of the door Roosevelt coolly remarked, 'Don't be foolish, Douglas; you and the budget must get together on this'. Dern came to him afterwards as they were walking out and gleefully told him, 'you've saved the Army'. MacArthur recalled in his memoirs: 'but I just vomited on the steps of the White House'.

After that stormy incident MacArthur reported that from then on Roosevelt was on the Army's side. MacArthur's resignation was not accepted and as a matter of fact, Roosevelt extended his term as Chief of Staff for one year in 1934, an unusual event at that time. Army appropriations were cut, but MacArthur managed with what he had by adopting a policy of limiting the army to development of pilot models of new equipment rather than committing itself to largescale manufacture of weapons that in the course of a short period of time would become obsolete. Such a policy had a great appeal in a country like the United States which was not likely to be invaded by land, and at a time when money was short. He realized that military plans and preparation take a number of years, but warned that a sufficient nucleus of an armed force must be maintained so that when danger threatened or when better economic prospects were in sight it could swiftly be built up again. His organizational reforms were cited upon his retirement as Chief of Staff in 1935, when he was awarded an Oak Leaf Cluster to his Distinguished Service Medal, for the creation of the nucleus of an Army Air Corps.

When he retired there was no place for MacArthur to go. It is more than likely that Roosevelt was happy to be rid of him so that a more like-minded individual could take his place. It was unfortunate for both MacArthur and Roosevelt that Manuel Quezon,

MacArthur's old friend from the Philippines, which had by now become a Commonwealth of the United States, had called on MacArthur in 1934 while he was still Chief of Staff. Commonwealth status in the American sense means a certain nominal independence, but with foreign affairs and major problems of defense as well as a few other reserve powers retained by the government in Washington. The Philippines had been told that this status would last for ten years, after which they could become independent. Quezon had initially called on MacArthur to discuss problems of Philippine national defense after the country had achieved independence. He asked if the islands were defensible. MacArthur replied that if sufficient money, men and munitions were made available as well as enough time to train the troops, provide the munitions and raise the money, any place is defensible. Quezon asked him if, upon his retirement as Chief of Staff, he would undertake the job and MacArthur replied that he would. But he also warned that it would take at least ten years with considerable help from the United States for the defense of the Philippines to be accomplished.

Soon after this meeting Roosevelt asked MacArthur to see him and told him that with the inauguration of the Commonwealth, the governor-generalship would lapse and be replaced by a high commissioner. The job could be his. This proposal would involve MacArthur's retirement from the army. MacArthur told the President that he had started as a soldier and wanted to end as one. A compromise was reached whereby MacArthur would do the job he was requested to do as a servant of the Philippine government, whose army would be developed independently of but in co-operation with the American garrison: the Philippine Department of

MacArthur arrives back in the Philippines in 1935. Colonel Eisenhower is behind him, to the left

the United States Army, which Mac-Arthur once headed. Its leader at that time, Major-General Lucius R Holbrook, was instructed to give all assistance possible to MacArthur.

At the age of fifty-five MacArthur was to embark upon a new career, but far enough away from Washington so that he could have no real political influence where it mattered. It could be said that Roosevelt wanted to maneuver MacArthur into this back-water, but in actual fact there was no place for MacArthur to go but the Philippines. He had an emotional and traditional attachment to the islands, and considered them his second home. It was a job which was likely to keep him busy until he was sixty-six, at which point, barring any unforeseen circumstances, he could retire to write his memoirs. MacArthur, however, did not consider the Philippines a backwater as Roosevelt might have done. He realized full well that a conflict in the Far East with Japan was only a matter of time, and that, out of a sense of loyalty to the island Commonwealth, he ought to do what he could to improve their defenses which he felt were imperative to the defense of the United States themselves. Before he left Washington, however, he re-established the Order of the Purple Heart, given to men wounded in action, a decoration which had not been used in over a century, and one which antedates almost all of the famous military medals in the world. It was one which was to be given many times before MacArthur left the Philippines again.

Just before he left for his new post MacArthur was given another medal of his own: his second Distinguished Service Medal. He sailed for the Philippines in the fall of 1935 on the *President Hoover* from San Francisco; his fifth tour in the Far East; and the most important mission in his life.

Manila before the storm

MacArthur's staff as Military Adviser of the Philippine Commonwealth consisted of four officers, among them Major D Eisenhower and James B Ord. Eisenhower greatly impressed MacArthur when he was on MacArthur's staff in Washington, and he and Ord helped draw up a plan for a Philippine National Defense Act, which intended to provide a militia of about 200,000 men organized into small divisions of about 7,500 each, a small air corps, and marines equipped with torpedo boats. With the reserve the total within ten years would come to about 400,000.

However, the plan ran into difficulties almost from the beginning. There was a movement afoot in the islands to reject the idea of national independence and to depend entirely upon the United States for defense, which Quezon and MacArthur crushed. There was a great deal of public doubt and apathy surrounding the project, and Quezon vigorously tried to combat this by telling his people that the only hope for peace in the Western Pacific was to rearm. Quezon had agreed with MacArthur that the Philippine government would provide 7.5 to 10 million dollars per annum to fulfill their military requirements. But Quezon was unable to meet these requirements. The budget dropped to only six million dollars and heavy opposition grew against the rearmament program. The rearmament proposals themselves had certain serious flaws. For one thing, there was no provision made for a battle fleet to protect the islands. MacArthur explained that since his mission was of a defensive character, only the interior waterways of the islands needed protection, which could be accomplished by torpedo boats, which could 'deny the enemy an opportunity to bring its forces close enough to Philippine shores to debark his troops and supplies'.

Dwight D Eisenhower (in 1930 a major)

James B Ord

The whole idea was mistaken from the start. To imagine that a few torpedo boats and a hundred bombers could prevent invasion of the dozens of islands of the Philippines by Japan was either naive or irresponsible. It is true to say that the Philippine government was unprepared to pay for the construction or purchase of a large defensive navy, but the fact that the United States was unprepared to defend the islands with its own under-equipped navy was hidden from the Philippine government and people. One could argue the point that since neither the American nor the Philippine government, because of the economic crisis and public apathy, could do much about making a realistic defense of the Philippines, the brave words emanating from time to time from MacArthur and Quezon would keep morale high. But one could counter that argument by stating that the disillusionment would be all the greater if the shaky defense program were ever put to the test, and that it helped create further apathy by lulling the population into thinking that everything was really all right. The best that can be said for Mac-Arthur's policy was that he contributed something to the defense of the

islands. But events were to prove that what was done was far from adequate, and that the exposure of the shores of the island Commonwealth to the huge Japanese Navy was downright scandalous. In MacArthur's defense one could say that whatever measures were taken they would have been inadequate anyway. But a more realistic attempt should have been made.

For example, the training of groups of recruits and then sending them home to train new groups was no way to form an effective army. A better plan might have been to train at least skeleton regiments and divisions from the start so that effective training could proceed at all levels. Even in this plan MacArthur lacked vision. He proposed an initial call-up of only 3,000, whereas Quezon insisted on the full quota of 20,000 in 1937. The result was that instructors were pretty thin on the ground, and the idea of saving money in the first years in order to be able to spend it later on did not work. The training of strong cadres prepared to fight would have taken large numbers of American officers and NCOs, which were not forthcoming from Washington. Intensive training of Filipino officers to fill the gap did not take place. MacArthur felt that half-trained cadres could tie the Japanese down to fighting protracted guerrilla warfare which could slow down their war effort if they launched a full-scale invasion of Southeast Asia and the Western Pacific. If the whole army were indoctrinated with guerrilla tactics from the start the plan might have been effective. But since they were not, the Philippine army could only prove a nuisance to a highly effective, well-equipped Japanese army invading by sea.

But the fault cannot be laid entirely at the feet of MacArthur. He noted that a certain coolness grew between Quezon and Roosevelt which made requests to Washington for aid all the

MacArthur's second marriage, in 1937, to Jean Faircloth

more difficult. Roosevelt, seeing the problem, offered MacArthur a new command which was to consist of the entire Pacific, including Hawaii and the American west coast. MacArthur refused, since he had promised Quezon that he would remain as adviser throughout Quezon's six-year term as President of the Commonwealth, which would end in 1943. Roosevelt's anger with MacArthur apparently was growing over the years. Their political philosophies were poles apart: their manner, though equally grandiose in style, had an important difference. Roosevelt got what he wanted through cunning and occasional guile. MacArthur's strong suit was hauteur and remoteness. The charm of his early years had gone. His mother, who had come with him to Manila, had died, and since his brother and father were gone, MacArthur was alone. He spent his spare time going to the movies almost every night and his remote disposition was intensified. His marriage to Jean Marie Faircloth in 1937 did much to alleviate this loneliness. The following year his son, Arthur, was born, and this renewal of family life did a lot for MacArthur, as he admitted himself. But the distance between him and his President was not narrowed by his new family responsibilities; the damage had been done and the rift was to widen.

In 1937 MacArthur made another trip, this time with Quezon to Japan, as well as Mexico and the United States, where MacArthur married his second wife. He was impressed and worried by Japan's obvious military build-up and the invasion of China proper was soon to begin. He realized at this point that in order to carry on their policy of expansion, the Japanese needed the oil and rubber of the Dutch East Indies as well as Malaya's tin and nickel not to mention the great rice basin of Burma and Thailand. The Philippines stood in the way of that expansion, and although there was little that the islands had which the

Japanese needed for their war effort, MacArthur believed that it was only a matter of time before the Japanese would try to seize the islands as part of a southward expansion policy. This need not necessarily have been the case; the Japanese might have bypassed the Philippines, but it stood to reason that if Japan planned to move southward one day, the Philippines would block the path. MacArthur was all the more determined to continue the military build-up of the islands. When he arrived in Washington he had to make a decision about taking up Roosevelt's offer to return to take command of the defense of Hawaii and the west coast. MacArthur, feeling that he was blocking the promotion of subordinates, took the step of retiring from the Army and being appointed field marshal of the Philippines, a rank which did not and still does not exist in the American Army, and a title which MacArthur dearly loved.

If MacArthur, the Philippine government and the American government did little to substantially improve the islands' defenses, at least MacArthur was able to improve morale. Acting on the assumption that grandeur impressed Asians, MacArthur succeeded in impressing the Filipinos with his sense of authority, if not infallibility. The pomp and ceremony of his unique office, the freedom to give full rein to his sense of the melodramatic, the gold braid and the new cap which he helped design himself, all served to create a public personality which slowly eradicated what was left of the genuine military hero of the First World War. MacArthur could get away with the sort of thing in Manila which would have raised eyebrows and sniggers in Washington. More important, the restraints naturally imposed upon him by his own government, by other high ranking members of the military élite and by the President were removed in his new status in the Philippines. His chief of staff, General

Richard K Sutherland, tended to ape the mannerisms of his superior. He was hard to handle, arrogant, autocratic and short-tempered, the wrong sort of person for the job. MacArthur did little or nothing to curb these tendencies in his chief of staff, and the atmosphere around MacArthur became more that of a court than a military headquarters.

This absorption of MacArthur's private personality by his public, or, rather, the merger of the two, struck many of his other subordinates as excessive. Major Eisenhower was one of them, and was recorded to have later remarked, when asked by a woman whether he had met MacArthur, 'Not only have I met him, madam, but I studied dramatics under him for five years in Washington and four in the Philippines'. He left MacArthur for another post during MacArthur's reign in Manila. Others like General Lewis H Brereton, were favorably impressed. He described MacArthur as 'one of the most beautiful talkers I have ever heard, and while his manner might be considered a bit on the theatrical side, it is just a part of his personality'. MacArthur had found a new role; one of acting the part of an absolute monarch: and one which he was to resume in Japan after the war.

The heady atmosphere of those Manila days before the Second World War and the lack of criticism of MacArthur which accompanied them was upset by the outbreak of war in Europe and the expansion of Japan's military involvement in China. By 1939 Japan had seized virtually the whole east coast of China facing the Philippines, and by mid-1940, after the fall of France and the Low Countries, Japan intensified her political and economic pressure on the isolated Dutch East Indies and invaded Tonking, now roughly the territory of North Vietnam, and then part of French Indo-China. The United States adopted a position of thinly disguised neutrality toward these actions, and worked

General Sutherland

behind the scenes to bolster the resolve of the French and Dutch colonial governments in Southeast Asia, achieving considerable success with respect to the latter, if not the former. A series of economic sanctions were imposed on Japan by the United States, which only encouraged Japan's resolve to expand into the rest of Southeast Asia, rather than acting as a deterrent, as the Americans presumably hoped.

It would have been sensible at this time for the Philippine government, acting on MacArthur's advice, to have called its armed forces together, or carried out a trial mobilization in order to test their organization. The new commander of the Philippine Department, Major-General George Grunert, was appointed in June, 1940 and he immediately asked for more men and equipment. Initially there was no response from Washington. Grunert pressed the point, arguing that the Philippine government no longer believed that the United States was prepared to defend the islands, and he recommended that a strong air and submarine force be established while US Army units built up and trained the Philippine Army. Quezon supported this request, but again no action was taken.

President Roosevelt had trouble enough in gaining the support necessary to introduce conscription, which finally passed the Congress in the autumn of 1940 and which permitted the United States to establish an army of almost a million and a half as well as the mobilization of the National Guard. The effect of isolationism was so strong that these measures were to be taken up for a year, after which they would be reviewed, and either continued and expanded, or ended. Although men on the spot like Grunert and MacArthur were aware of the inherent dangers of the growing crisis, and their view was shared by Roosevelt and a sizeable minority in Congress and among the American people, disillusion, which had swept the United States after the First World War, still had its after-effects, and organizations like the American First Committee and proto-fascist groups fanned the flames of isolationism.

Roosevelt wanted to help, but there was little he could do other than the actions which he did take. The trouble was, however, that Roosevelt's main concern was with Europe, not Asia. He believed that the take-over of Western Europe by Hitler posed a greater danger to American security than the Japanese take-over of Northern Indo-China. There are few people today who would doubt Roosevelt's judgement. But there were many at that time who did, who resented the fact that when Lend-Lease was finally enacted, most of the aid went to Britain, and very little to the Pacific area; that when the destroyer-base deal was concluded, the naval assistance went to secure Britain in the North Atlantic and in the North Sea, rather than to Singapore or Hong Kong. Isolationists tended to thinly disguise a definable Anglophobia and, sometimes, a certain recognition of the advantages a Nazi-controlled European continent would offer. These same groups and individuals, on the other hand, tended to stress the importance of the Pacific as a primary area of American interest, rather than a decadent and ungrateful Europe. MacArthur was more in this camp than in the camp of Roosevelt and the Europe-firsters, and this was another cause of the rift between Roosevelt and MacArthur that was to increasingly damage America's Far Eastern posture.

In all fairness, however, it must be mentioned that America was just beginning its military build-up in 1940, that priorities had to be given for the limited resources America had at its disposal at that time. Roosevelt, after all, chose the right priority, however desirable it might have been to be able to train the American Army at home, develop the necessary material of war, supply Britain and later, Russia, with whatever could be spared, rearm and re-equip an out-of-date navy and a virtually non-existent air corps and, at the same time, supply the Philippines with arms, men, training, and a fleet. The Philippines were toward the bottom of America's list of priorities. The Dutch East Indies, with the oil and rubber and tin which the United States so desperately needed and which Japan coveted, could be supplied with little or nothing from America's growing but still small storehouse of weapons and ships. The American government urged the Netherlands Indies government to resist Japanese demands for more goods, but could do little more than that. And the Dutch East Indies were far more important, strategically and in terms of natural resources, to the United States and its defense than their own Commonwealth was. Small wonder that MacArthur and Grunert were disappointed in Roosevelt's lack of response to their requests.

Yet further requests were forthcoming from Manila. In November 1940 General George C Marshall in Washington was told by Grunert that the Philippine Army possessed twelve divisions comprising 120,000 trained

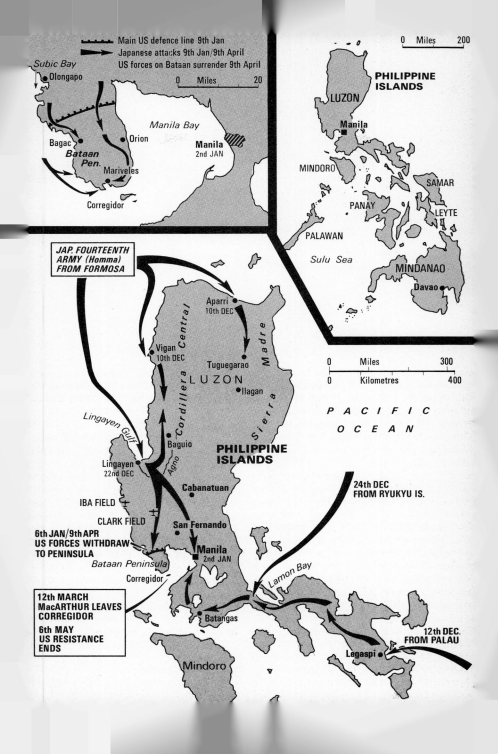

Main US defence line 9th Jan
Japanese attacks 9th Jan/9th April
US forces on Bataan surrender 9th April

0   Miles   20

Subic Bay
Olongapo

Manila Bay

Manila
2nd JAN

Bagac
Bataan Pen.
Orion

Mariveles

Corregidor

0   Miles   200

PHILIPPINE ISLANDS

LUZON

Manila

MINDORO

SAMAR

PANAY

LEYTE

PALAWAN

Sulu Sea

MINDANAO

Davao

JAP. FOURTEENTH ARMY (Homma) FROM FORMOSA

Aparri
10th DEC

Vigan
10th DEC

Tuguegarao

Cordillera Central

L U Z O N

Ilagan

Sierra Madre

Lingayen Gulf

Baguio

Lingayen
22nd DEC

Agno

PHILIPPINE ISLANDS

Cabanatuan

IBA FIELD

CLARK FIELD

6th JAN/9th APR US FORCES WITHDRAW TO PENINSULA

San Fernando

Bataan Peninsula

Manila
2nd JAN

Corregidor

12th MARCH MacARTHUR LEAVES CORREGIDOR

6th MAY US RESISTANCE ENDS

Batangas

Lamon Bay

0   Miles   300
0   Kilometres   400

P A C I F I C

O C E A N

24th DEC
FROM RYUKYU IS.

12th DEC.
FROM PALAU

Legaspi

Mindoro

men, but made it clear that the bulk of these were in reserve and not on active duty. About half of the officers, however, had no training and no unit larger than a battalion had ever been assembled for field training; it was a paper army. Grunert proposed that, in the event of an attack, Filipinos should be used in companies and battalions with an American officer commanding each company. He also recommended that Filipino units be mobilized immediately and asked for 500 officers. In response to this request seventy-five were sent and the proposal to mobilize the army was rejected due to lack of funds. By the first of the year, however, Washington relented a little; it was decided to send sixty field artillery weapons and twenty old anti-aircraft guns as reinforcements.

Despite these pitiful responses MacArthur held an optimistic view. He stated that the Philippines would be able to defend themselves if given enough time; the target date was 1946.

Above: In full finery, with President Quezon, Manila, July 1941. *Right:* Charles A Lindbergh addresses an America First anti-war rally

He suggested that it would cost an enemy at least a half a million casualties and 'upwards of five billion dollars' to succeed in invading the islands. In a letter to Marshall in February 1941 he described his mission as one of preparing the Philippines to be able to resist an enemy attack by 1946, and that the planned army of a quarter of a million men would be ready by the end of 1941. This, plus his small air force and thirty to fifty motor torpedo boats, he reckoned, could provide 'an adequate defense at the beach against a landing operation by an expeditionary force of 100,000 which is estimated to be the maximum initial effort of the most powerful potential enemy'.

MacArthur envisaged defending not only Manila Bay and Luzon but the Visayas as well (the central islands of

the Philippines) by blocking the straits leading to its inland seas. Therefore, he reported that he would need seven 12-inch guns, twenty-five 155-mm guns and thirty-two mobile searchlights. He was told that the heavy guns would not be available until 1943 and the medium guns and searchlights not until 1942. Even these feeble efforts, which appear optimistic to say the least to repel a heavily armed and prepared Japanese invader, were thwarted by Washington. When asked to comment, Grunert repeated the fact that the Philippine Army 'had practically no field training nor target practice'. The Philippine defense force had, at this time, forty-two aircraft and two torpedo boats. The Philippines were a sitting duck.

In April 1941 staff talks were held between British, American and Netherlands Indies officers to plan the defense of Southeast Asia against what they presumed to be an inevitable Japanese attack. The assumption

again was made, with the unenthusiastic and begrudged approval of her Allies, that the United States, which potentially had the most to offer the area in the way of specific arms, planes and ships, would concentrate its war effort (once America was in the war: this too was presumed) on victory in Europe rather than Asia. A defensive posture, a holding operation, was the most that could be hoped for in the Western Pacific.

These Singapore talks suggested that the defenses of Luzon be strengthened and that a bomber force be created there so that a bombing offensive could later be launched against the home islands of Japan. General Grunert remarked afterwards that 'our present mission and restrictions as to means are not in accord' with this report. By this time the decision had been reached to move some of the American Pacific fleet to the Atlantic so that the ratio between the Atlantic and Pacific fleets would be 60:40. Furthermore,

FDR signs the Lend-Lease Bill, 1941

the defense of Singapore was to be left in the hands of the British and the Dutch, neither of whom had sufficient weapons and ships to realistically forestall a full-scale Japanese attack. The American fleet was to be largely withdrawn to Pearl Harbor.

Whether they realized it or not, the Allies had by now decided to draw a line of defense across the International Date Line, and those Allied-held areas to the west of that line would have to fend for themselves in the best way they could. Reports coming from the area, including the Philippines suggested that if any sort of defense were possible, it would be a holding action, which the Allies hoped would tie Japanese forces down to the extent that they would be unable to threaten Hawaii or, at least, the west coast of the United States, Australia and New Zealand until sufficient arms had been built up in the States to throw back the invader. Even this plan was overly optimistic; without massive American support, logistically and otherwise, the area of Southeast Asia could not repel a full-scale attack from Japan.

The situation appeared more bleak when virtually all hopes for a Japanese attack on Russia rather than Southeast Asia faded when Japan made a non-aggression pact with the Soviet Union. Unaware that Hitler was planning a summer offensive against his new ally, Russia, the Japanese had opted for a southern strategy; that is, if the peace negotiations with America and economic negotiations with the Dutch East Indies did not bear fruit. In July, 1941, the American Chief of Naval Operations, Admiral Harold R Stark, and General Marshall rejected the report of the Singapore meeting; the United States was not going to reinforce the Philippines because 'of the greater needs of other strategic areas'. They continued, 'under present world conditions, it is considered possible to hope to launch a strong offensive from the Philippines'.

Already in May MacArthur had received a letter from Marshall, the chief of staff. He suggested that MacArthur become Army Commander in the Far East 'should the situation approach a crisis'. He explained that the Secretary of War felt that the time had not yet come when such an appointment could be made, but wanted to inform MacArthur so that when the time came he was prepared and the President was ready to approve such an appointment. In June MacArthur told Washington that he proposed to close the office of Military Adviser since he anticipated that the American Army would absorb the Philippine Army shortly. MacArthur agreed to accept the appointment of commander of all the armies in the Far East. By July the War Department accepted and enlarged upon proposals made by MacArthur. The Philippine Army would be absorbed into the American; 425 reserve officers would be sent out to the Commonwealth from the United States; and MacArthur would be recalled to active duty and given command of the combined army and air force. The

US troops in the Philippines.
Reinforcements were hard to get

60

Secretary of War, former governor-general of the Philippines Henry L Stimson, approved. On 26th July 1941 MacArthur was given the command.

It is interesting to note that just before this appointment was made the Japanese moved into southern Indo-China and that weeks before that, the Japanese negotiations with the Dutch in Batavia, capital of the Dutch East Indies, had broken down; the Dutch had refused to fulfill the lavish requests made by Japan for strategic raw materials, although they had come some of the way toward a settlement. On 26th July, the day of MacArthur's appointment, the United States, followed almost immediately by Britain and Holland, froze Japanese assets in their respective areas. The Allies knew that this act, which would not allow Japan supplies she needed to continue the war in China, much less allow her to persevere in actions

**A military review in Manila, 1941.
MacArthur remained falsely optimistic**

anywhere else, was tantamount to a declaration of war. It was now only a matter of counting the days until she either backed down, which seemed highly unlikely, or went to war. MacArthur was given the rank of major-general, but the next day was promoted to lieutenant-general; five months later he regained the rank of general.

As commander of United States Army Forces in the Far East (USAFFE) MacArthur formed a new staff, comprising many members of his old team, which remained largely intact throughout the course of the war. Sutherland stayed on as his chief of staff and his senior intelligence officer was Lieutenant-Colonel Charles A Willoughby, who was to lead his intelligence team from then on and who was, incidentally, a naturalized American of German origin. MacArthur's initial plan was to defend Manila Bay above all until reinforcements could arrive; this was similar to Britain's position in Singapore.

There were those who criticized this plan, critics who felt that defending the Philippines was a waste of energy and manpower, and that the United States would do better by acquiescing in the temporary loss of their Commonwealth. Australians felt that Singapore had insufficient defenses and that it was vulnerable on the landward side. MacArthur however worked on the presumption that although he still needed five more years for the Philippines to be impregnable, he could put up a decent defense of the islands. Realizing that his weakest element was the air, he sought to establish a supply link of airfields stretching from lower Mindanao to upper Luzon which would be connected with airfields in Australia, the Dutch East Indies and Malaya. By October nine new B-17 bombers had arrived at Clark Field outside Manila as well as fifty pursuit planes. By December, however, American operational air forces totalled only thirty-five bombers and seventy-two pursuit planes, less than half of what MacArthur felt was necessary. Even his hoped-for total was far short of what was required. But on the seas, over which MacArthur had no direct authority, the situation was pitifully weak, even worse than the lack of air strength. The entire fleet was composed of three cruisers, thirteen destroyers eighteen submarines and six PT boats.

MacArthur's assessment still included a fairly optimistic appraisal of the coming crisis. He expected that the Japanese would land with a force of about 100,000 men, and that they would make a surprise attack on the islands somewhere around December 1941 or January 1942. American efforts would concentrate on preventing them from landing, but if this failed the defending army would be withdrawn to the Bataan Pensinula, the key to the control of Manila Bay and the last redoubt of the American forces. The plan presumed that Japanese forces could be held long enough for reinforcements to reach Bataan, which was supposed to be able to hold off the Japanese for 180 days, after which the American forces, if not reinforced, would be forced to capitulate. This plan, however, was soon abandoned and replaced with a new one, which also rejected another scheme, Rainbow 5, which implicitly accepted the loss of the Philippines and which recognized Germany as the principal opponent of the United States. Major-General Lewis Brereton arrived with the plan on 3rd November when he came to Manila to take command of MacArthur's air force. It was a letter from Marshall authorizing MacArthur to defend the whole archipelago. MacArthur welcomed this news, without recognizing the impossibility of putting the new plan into effect. MacArthur tended to underestimate the Japanese and seized upon any information he heard which tended to presume Japan's weakness or war-weariness from her struggle in China.

What caused the change of heart in Washington? One reason was undoubtedly MacArthur's continued optimism, as expressed in his reports to Washington. If he, with all his experience and knowledge of the situation on the spot, felt that the islands could be defended, Washington was not going to stand in his way. The other reason could have been the astounding success of American Flying Fortresses operating against Germany from Britain. But, as MacArthur reported himself, there were only thirty-five bombers in the Philippines by December. In October Secretary of War Stimson told the Secretary of State, Cordell Hull, that time was needed to prepare the islands; three months. And at this point there were less than two months to go. By December there were only sixty-one of the heavy bombers, the B-17s, at American bases outside the United States and not many more existed in the States. There were less than two dozen B-17s in Britain at this time.

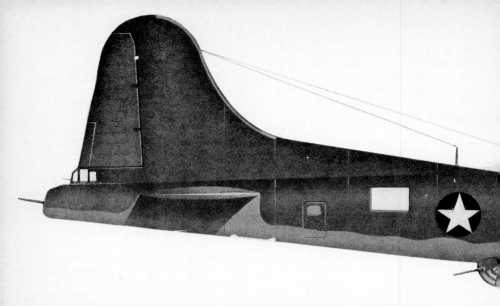

Boeing B-17F *Engines:* four Wright R-1820, 1,200 hp each at 25,000 feet.
Armament: up to twelve .5-inch Browning machine guns and 8,000 lbs of bombs.
Speed: 299 mph at 25,000 feet. *Ceiling:* 37,000. *Range:* 1.300 miles with a 6,000 lbs
bomb load. *Weight empty/loaded:* 34,000/56,500 lbs. *Span:* 103 feet 9 inches.
Length: 74 feet 9 inches. *Crew:* 10

Thus, based largely on MacArthur's optimism alone, a group of obsolete aircraft supported by a few modern ones, a navy which hardly existed at all, and an army which was ill-prepared and which consisted of not more than about 22,000 men under arms was preparing to take on the strength of Imperial Japan. Even by comparison with the British force in Malaya at this time, which did not prove equal to the task, the American force in the Phillipines was weak.

MacArthur decided to mobilize his reserves, but since there were not enough quarters to accommodate the 75,000 men of the ten reserve divisions, he then decided to call his reserves up in contingents between September and 15th December, when the mobilization would be complete. MacArthur organized his forces into four commands: the North Luzon Force under Major-General Jonathan Wainwright, which would be deployed in Luzon north of Manila; the South Luzon Force under Brigadier-General George M Parker, Jr, which would defend the rest of the island; the Visayan-Mindanao Force under Brigadier-General William F Sharp, which was supposed to defend the rest of the archipelago; and forces under Major-General George F Moore, which commanded the harbor defenses in Manila and Subic Bays. A general reserve force including the Philippine Division of the US Army and the remaining Philippine division of the Philippine Army was placed in an area around Manila. Wainwright, therefore, with little more than four ill-equipped and under-trained divisions had to defend an area about 300 miles long where the enemy attacks were expected. MacArthur ordered Wainwright not to withdraw from the beach positions which were to be held 'at all costs'. The artillery to be used was largely of First World War vintage, and artillery support was a small fraction of what was usual at the time and

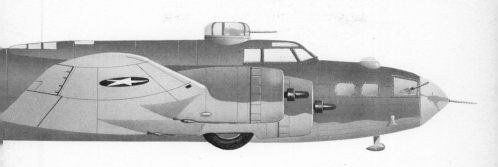

about one-third of the strength established for the Philippine Division. Motor vehicles were scarce; even personal equipment was in short supply.

The continued optimism of MacArthur, even in these last days, leads one to believe either that he did not know what was going on, which was doubtful, or that the staff knew and were afraid to tell MacArthur. This conclusion is dubious, however. MacArthur reports in his memoirs that he knew that he was short of material, but believed that the will of the Philippine people and the intensity of the resistance of his forces gave him a chance to hold the islands until reinforcements arrived from the States. It is pretty certain that MacArthur did not know the enormity of the problems facing his forces. It is more than likely that he had convinced himself that his luck would hold and that, somehow, the invincible image that he tirelessly constructed

in the islands since 1935 was a true image of the man who could hold off any foe. MacArthur later blamed Washington for having let him down. But he knew that Washington and particularly the President were of the opinion that the principal enemy was Germany, and that whatever crumbs he could expect after the fighting began would be insufficient to hold the islands for more than a few months, at most. It is more probable that he was kidding himself all along and, worst of all, kidding the Philippine people.

Even at the last political problems dogged MacArthur's footsteps. It had been proposed that MacArthur be given command of the naval forces in the area as well, but Admiral Thomas C Hart, commanding the US Asiatic Fleet, which consisted of two cruisers, plus some destroyers, submarines and small craft, insisted that these forces remain under his control. MacArthur objected vehemently, and relations

between Hart and MacArthur deteriorated. Furthermore MacArthur still held out the hope that the Japanese would by-pass the Philippines in order to avoid fighting the United States, and concentrate instead on seizing British and Dutch possessions in Southeast Asia. Although historians now know that this idea was discussed in the presence of the Emperor it was rejected; it was not unrealistic of MacArthur to have thought of this possibility, however.

MacArthur was also ordered not to initiate any action until the Japanese opened hostilities; the first overt moves were to come from the enemy. Therefore, it must have occurred to Roosevelt and Marshall that the Philippines might be by-passed. But certainly for reasons of convincing American public opinion that demanded a direct attack on American territory if it were to be fully convinced that America should go to war, Roosevelt hoped that when the attack came, it would come on the Philippines. This move was contemplated months before and it was for this reason that American naval power, such as it was, was almost completely recalled to Pearl Harbor, where the Americans felt it would be safe from Japanese attack. To have left the American Pacific Fleet in the Philippines without adequate air cover would have made it an open target when the Japanese attack came.

MacArthur could not have known that Roosevelt had given his word to the Dutch that if the Japanese attacked the Dutch East Indies alone, without hitting the Philippines, the United States would come to the aid of the Dutch. One thing is certain: the Japanese thought very little of MacArthur's defense schemes. Japanese intelligence, which was amazingly accurate, and which had been collected over several years by Japanese civilians operating within the islands as well as through the more usual

channels, had a thorough knowledge of American strength in the Philippines. The Japanese Fourteenth Army was allotted only two divisions to accomplish its projected conquest of the Philippines. Lieutenant-General Homma would have powerful naval cover and the support of some 500 planes. He was instructed to complete his conquest of the islands within fifty days, after which part of his forces would be deployed to help in the attack on Java, one of Japan's principal targets. The Japanese estimate was pretty close to the mark, and in many respects was pessimistic; the forces which took the Philippines were not even needed on Java, which fell at almost the same time as the Commonwealth did. It just took a little longer than the Japanese figured.

The question which remains is this: was MacArthur set up for a defeat? Of course, it is unthinkable that the President of the United States would willfully desire American territory to fall into the hands of the enemy. But every indication is that Roosevelt and his generals in Washington had no choice but to accept the inevitable. American public opinion, even on the eve of war, was not fully convinced of the dangers which Germany and Japan posed to the security of the United States. But it is also likely that Roosevelt was not anxious to have a victorious MacArthur on his hands; win the war he would; but the glory would not go to MacArthur. There could be no glory in an unsuccessful holding operation, and this was the role set out for MacArthur, whether he wanted it or not.

Was MacArthur irresponsible in convincing the American government that there was any hope of defending the Philippines? It is fairly certain that the attempts MacArthur made in this direction were not successful. Faced with the lack of supplies available to the American government at this time, largely because of the hostility of a large body of public opinion to rearmament in the Thirties,

Major-General Jonathan Wainwright

67

Major-General Lewis H Brereton

Major-General George F Moore

Admiral Thomas C Hart

Cordell Hull, US Secretary of State

Brigadier-General George M Parker

General Homma

there was little more the American government could have done. It would have done no good at all to have had MacArthur face the Philippine people with the desperate nature of their plight. The atmosphere among the British, Dutch and American communities in the Far East just before the Pearl Harbor attack was a strange combination of heady, unrealistic optimism and a deep-seated, racist-inspired, opinion that whatever the military and naval position, the Japanese, a short, squinty-eyed, inscrutible Oriental people, simply could not defeat the Westerners.

It was an opinion, strangely enough, that was shared by many native Southeast Asians. The reputation of the invincible Westerner had been built up for almost a century, perhaps more, in the minds of millions of Southeast Asians, and MacArthur set himself up as the archetype of this model. Japan might be able to defeat a decadent Imperial Russia, all right; they might be capable of defeating the Chinese. But they simply could not defeat the Americans, British and Dutch. This was the prevailing mood. When that mood was shattered in three months, when the prestige of the West meant nothing against military, air and naval superiority, Japan had wrecked a spiritual edifice which could never be re-established. MacArthur shared this mood and helped to spread it throughout the territories under his command. In that sense MacArthur was irresponsible, but no more so than his counterparts in British and Dutch-controlled territories. Worst of all, in the atmosphere of infallibility which he created among his own staff, he was able to convince himself that he could defeat Japan, or at least hold her for a long time; and by convincing himself, he was able to successfully convince too many others. The rude, brutal awakening was to come as a shock when Japan's air force shattered Pearl Harbor on the morning of 7th December 1941.

The warrior defeated

In late November, 1941 MacArthur received reports from Admiral Hart and General Marshall that there was little prospect that an agreement would be reached with Japan and that Japanese troop movements indicated the likelihood of an attack in any direction. It was clear that an overt attack could take place at any moment, but MacArthur was again warned not to make the first move, but that this should not be construed to mean that MacArthur should not do everything in his power to make the island ready for attack short of making a pre-emptive strike himself. On 28th November the Navy Department sent the commanders of the Pacific and Asiatic fleets a 'war warning' which stated that an aggressive move by Japan was to be expected within the next few days. MacArthur cabled Marshall telling him that everything was in readiness. Reports that Japanese ships were moving towards Malaya and unidentified aircraft appearing over Luzon

strengthened this belief. MacArthur ordered Wainwright to be ready at any moment. It was expected that if an attack occurred on American territory it would be on the Philippines.

At half past three on the morning (Philippine time) of 8th December General Sutherland heard over the radio that Pearl Harbor was being attacked by Japanese planes. He telephoned MacArthur at once, and it was not until two hours later that MacArthur was officially informed that America was at war with Japan, although at 3.40 he had received a telephone call from Washington informing him that Japan had attacked Hawaii. MacArthur's first impression was that Japan would suffer a serious defeat at Pearl Harbor. He awaited reports of a simultaneous attack on the Philippines.

There was only one radar station operative in the islands. At half

MacArthur and Wainwright in October 1941

past nine reconnaissance planes reported a force of enemy bombers over Lingayen Gulf heading toward Manila. Brereton ordered pursuit planes up to intercept them, but the enemy bombers veered off without making contact with the Americans. Instead they turned north and attacked Baguio, the summer capital, and other targets. MacArthur was still under the impression that Japan had suffered a setback at Pearl Harbor, and concluded that the Japanese planes veered off because they had received word of a Japanese defeat. Sometime between half past nine and half past eleven however, MacArthur learned the truth; much to his astonishment, the Japanese had achieved a smashing victory over American forces in Hawaii, who were taken by surprise despite the warnings given.

At 11.45 MacArthur received a report that an overpowering enemy formation of planes was closing in on Clark Field, America's principal air base in the islands. America had only two air fields which could handle the big B-17 bombers, which were MacArthur's only really strong card: Clark Field, north of Manila, and Del Monte, 800 miles to the south in Mindanao. Two of the four squadrons of B-17s had been removed to Del Monte some days before the war broke out in order to keep them out of danger. But the rest were on the ground at Clark. Brereton proposed that these B-17s be sent into the air at once to make a strike against Japanese Formosa. This proposal was put to MacArthur on three occasions on the morning of the 8th, but MacArthur refused to act in each instance. From 8am onwards the bombers were in the air but without any bombs. MacArthur ordered an attack on Formosa for the afternoon, so at half past eleven the bombers were back on the ground at Clark being armed. The Japanese planes, however, the main force consisting of 108 bombers and eighty-four Zeros (fighter planes),

were delayed by fog from taking off from Formosa, and did not leave until 10.15. Within an hour and a half they were over Clark and Iba field. When the attack was over the United States had lost 18 of its 35 B-17s in the Philippines, 53 fighters and 25–30 other aircraft. Only seven Japanese fighters had been lost in the attack.

There can be little doubt that MacArthur lost the Philippines in the first hours of the war. Had the bombers taken off armed from Clark at once, they could have made a strike against Formosa before the Japanese were in the air with their main strike force. MacArthur later denied any knowledge of the fact that Brereton had made the proposal that the American bombers take off for Formosa immediately. He claimed that the proposals had been made to Sutherland, not to him, and that they should have been made to him. It would be useless to try to place blame in this way. The fact remains that MacArthur was in charge and, even if the proposals had not been made to him personally, he should have thought of the idea and, at least, done something to protect his only really effective weapon, his bombers.

MacArthur argued later that the bombers would have had insufficient fighter cover, and that the effort, if made, would have been suicidal. Yet he did authorize the bombers to leave in the afternoon, after the fog over Formosa had lifted and after the enemy planes had already made their way to the Philippines. Even if he had not decided to send the bombers to Formosa, he could at least have flown them to Del Monte, where they could have been used later on. Their flight over the Philippines unarmed, only to return to Clark to be armed, was futile. It was a disastrous error on MacArthur's part, for which he and the American forces were to pay dearly. But after the morning of the 8th, it was clear that the Americans had lost the Philippines, and what was to occur subsequently was merely a tragic epilogue to the initial error.

It still might be mentioned in MacArthur's defense that his directive from Washington specifically stated that he should make no overt move against the enemy until they had done so first. Therefore, this would seem to preclude a strike against Formosa. But since Japanese planes were sighted over Luzon at 9.30, the order to strike could have been given at that time. There could be little doubt that the United States was at war with Japan after news came in the early morning hours that Pearl Harbor had been attacked. What further incentive was needed for MacArthur to have acted?

Perhaps a strike against Formosa might have made some difference in the long-term result; it might have delayed the Japanese for a while. But the overwhelming air and naval superiority which Japan had could not have been repelled in the long run. The initial air raids on Luzon were followed by Japanese landings at points somewhat remote from Manila: Aparri and Vigan in the north on 10th December and Legaspi in the south on the 12th. MacArthur believed that these landings were made with the idea of establishing airfields from which to cover other major landings which were to be made later on. But Japanese confidence was high, and they felt they could take the islands with a small number of men landing from Formosa in the north and from Palau Island in the south, which had been heavily and increasingly fortified in the last two years.

MacArthur believed that he could last for a considerable period as long as reinforcements which he counted on were forthcoming. Back in Washington the War Department was shaken by the disastrous news from Pearl Harbor. Most of the Pacific Fleet had been destroyed at a stroke. Roosevelt and Stimson were not of a mind to send what remaining forces they had three or four thousand miles west of their forward base against what they knew to be superior enemy forces just to save MacArthur's bacon in the Philippines. The islands, in their view, were not worth the effort based on the strength which America then had. But MacArthur felt that the navy could and should deliver a counter-offensive against Japan immediately; he suggested a bold stroke which might have had some effect: to send a group of carriers against the home islands which would force Japan to withdraw from the areas they were now attacking. This move certainly would have raised morale in the Philippines and the States, but whether it would have been successful or not is another matter. Moving imaginary fleets across a map may create a smug atmosphere at headquarters, but such actions are pointless when one cannot deliver the goods. The only two capital ships the Allies had in the Western Pacific, the British battleship *Prince of Wales* and its sister battle cruiser *Repulse*, were sunk off the Malayan coast on 10th December; without sufficient air cover they were sitting targets for the Japanese.

MacArthur still believed reinforcements would be sent. In fact a convoy of seven vessels escorted by the cruiser *Pensacola* was on its way to Manila when the war broke out. The convoy was carrying a field artillery brigade with twenty 75mm guns, eighteen P-40s, fifty-two A-24 dive bombers and considerable supplies of ammunition. On 12th December the convoy was re-routed to Brisbane. MacArthur complained bitterly to Hart about this, but Hart, according to MacArthur, was of the opinion that the Philippines were doomed. At roughly this time MacArthur also asked for 250 dive bombers and 300 fighters which, he suggested, could be flown in from aircraft carriers. Marshall assured him that some aircraft would be sent to the Philippines, but the bulk would go to Brisbane. By 13th December MacArthur was telling Marshall that the decision to concentrate the war effort on Germany first should be reversed and that all avail-

Pearl Harbor. US battleships after the Japanese attack

able reinforcements should be used against Japan. This course of action was rejected, of course, and none of the *Pensacola* convoy's men or material ever got to the Philippines. Although two vessels were sent forward from Brisbane, they were diverted to Darwin and some artillery units were used in Java.

MacArthur showed a complete lack of understanding of America's capabilities at this time, and disagreed violently with her 'Europe first' policy, as he always had done. The brilliant tactician and leader of men of the First World War was politically out of touch with his government and most of his fellow senior generals. Although American public opinion was shocked and embittered by the Pearl Harbor disaster, only a few die-hard remnants of the America-First, quasi-isolationist clique still supported a 'defeat Japan

first' policy. MacArthur, though out of close contact with the United States for some time, could have surmised this, but he was so wrapped up in his own affairs that he lost sight of America's primary objective. Worst of all, his tactical ability failed him, and his overestimation of America's present strength caused him to ask the Chief of Staff for equipment that America did not have or, at least, was unwilling to give to a cause which they felt was lost from the beginning.

The mobilization of Filipino manpower, however, was a success. By 8th December it was almost complete and some units were even overstrength; new units were formed out of the surplus, including two regiments and two battalions of artillery. Despite this strength in manpower, MacArthur recognized on the 12th that his original plan of defending the whole of the archipelago could not be accomplished. He informed President Quezon that if the Japanese landed in strength he would concentrate his forces on the

Bataan Peninsula outside Manila and withdraw his headquarters and the government to Corregidor at the tip of the peninsula; in short, that he was returning to War Plan Orange which had been the accepted one until four months before. This would mean that Manila would be declared an open city. It was probably at this point that MacArthur began to realize that the game was up and that the only effect resistance would have would be to delay the inevitable Japanese victory. MacArthur was then faced with the task of transporting quantities of ammunition and food to Bataan to prepare for the siege, to withdraw his Luzon forces into the peninsula, and to establish a defensive position across the neck of Bataan. MacArthur, however, delayed the decision to withdraw to Bataan until after the main Japanese landings had taken place, thereby losing further time and postponing what he knew had to be done. Again indecision and bad timing were to cost the Americans and Filipinos heavily.

General Count Terauchi's Southern Army had been charged with the attack on Allied-held Southeast Asia. Four armies were organized for the assault, one of which, the Fourteenth, composed of two divisions, one brigade and one regimental group, was earmarked to take the Philippines. Lieutenant-General Homma's Fourteenth Army included the 48th Division, two of whose regiments were Formosan, and the 16th Division. One of the Formosan regiments had made the initial landing in northern Luzon, while two battalions of the 16th Division plus a battalion of marines, had made the first landing in southern Luzon. Homma, therefore, had four infantry divisions left. He sent three of these and two regiments of tanks to Lingayen Gulf and the rest to the south.

At first glance this force did not seem formidable opposition to the defenders who had at least nine divisions under arms. But the lack of

naval reinforcements and air power was to make all the difference. The main Japanese force was to land along a twenty mile front and then fan out northwards to link with the forces already on Luzon. MacArthur had expected an attack at about this spot within a fortnight after the decision was made to withdraw to Bataan; that is, on or about 28th December. At dawn on the 22nd the invasion began in a storm which caused the loss of many landing craft. The second wave of landing forces was also delayed, but once ashore made short work of the ill-trained Philippine troops. There was no successful American bombardment of the landing, and General Homma decided to press forward against the advice of some of his staff. MacArthur's hopes that, despite their lack of training the Filipino troops could put up a stalwart defense, were dashed from the outset. He reported that they had broken at the first appearance of the enemy. The 71st Division, despite some reinforcements, fled the following day from their position across the Rosario road, which was to block their route toward the south and Manila. That same day Wainwright received permission to withdraw behind the Agno River, which crossed the Japanese route to Manila. If Wainwright could hold this position for any length of time, the Bataan fortress could complete its preparations and acquire sufficient supplies to maintain itself even under a long and heavy siege. MacArthur wisely sent most of his well-trained Philippine Division to Bataan at this stage. By this time Marshall had approved MacArthur's plan to declare Manila an open city and to withdraw to the peninsula.

On Christmas Day Admiral Hart left the Philippines to join his main force, which had already left and was now in the Dutch East Indies. Brereton was now in Darwin with his bomber force. All that was left of the remaining naval forces were six motor torpedo boats, a few other small vessels, and a few

Above: American Wildcat fighters lie wrecked after the Japanese attack on the Philippine airfields. *Below:* A ruined B-17 at Hickam Field, Hawaii. Many suffered a similar fate in the Philippines. *Right:* USS Pensacola

subs, which were soon to leave as well. In little more than a fortnight MacArthur's high hopes for defending the islands had collapsed; MacArthur and Wainwright were left to stave off the inevitable with little more than a brave band of American troops and indifferent support from their paper army of Philippine soldiers.

On 24th December the Japanese invasion of Southern Luzon met with equal success. By the end of their first day the Japanese had crossed the island and were prepared to move north and westward toward Manila. Unless Wainwright's line could hold

Manila would be surrounded. By Christmas night Wainwright had been pushed back to the Agno River. The American lines held for two nights, as the Japanese awaited the arrival of more artillery. By the 28th the defenders had given up their first two positions and were back to their last lines of defense. MacArthur, who reported that his men were tired but still had the situation well in hand, was forced to supply them by using commercial buses and private motor vehicles, as there were not enough military vehicles to do the job. Wainwright was still told to hang on

as long as he could and then withdraw, while the engineers dynamited bridges and roads as they retreated.

General Homma, however, upset the American plans by attempting to cut across to block the retreat into Bataan, but he had been ordered to take Manila, despite the fact that he knew that MacArthur himself had already gone to Corregidor. Instead of pressing on toward Bataan, he sent the bulk of his forces toward Manila and only sent a regimental group toward Bataan. This move allowed the Americans to continue their withdrawal. Meanwhile, the main contingents of the south Luzon Force were hurriedly making their way northward, and within seven days had withdrawn 140 miles through very rugged country. The rearguard which was holding the roads along the retreat route made a sharp counteroffensive which cost the Japanese eight tanks and which thereafter slowed their advance. By the first of January most of the organized troops were either in Bataan

or near San Fernando on the road back. Homma's army pressed towards an undefended Manila, which was taken on the following day.

The rearguard made its way to Bataan within the next five days, harrassed by Japanese forces as it withdrew. The withdrawal had not been unsuccessful, but 13,000 troops were lost in the process, most of them deserters; dispirited Filipinos from Wainwright's force. The supply buildup on Bataan, however, was less successful. The war plans had called for supplies for 43,000 men for six months, but due to MacArthur's delay in issuing the order to retreat to Bataan, this was not achieved. Corregidor had rations for 10,000 men for six months, but Bataan had only enough for 100,000 men for thirty days. The crowded and chaotic conditions

in the beleaguered peninsula called for more than even the war plans had foreseen. There were not 43,000 men there now, but 80,000, and there were over 25,000 civilian refugees. Before the last troops entered the fortress MacArthur reduced the daily rations to half their normal amount for civilians and soldiers alike, about 2,000 calories.

Homma's troops were to be reduced because of orders received which asked him to release his best group, the 48th Division, for action in Java, which according to the original Japanese timetable was not to be invaded for at least another month. Japan now felt confident enough to ship these forces southwards and replace them with the six battalions of the 65th Brigade. In opposition to this reduced Japanese force Mac-Arthur still had two regular Philippine Army divisions and seven Philippine Army reserve divisions, which, if they could have been given reinforcements or even enough food and ammunition,

Above: **General Homma coming ashore in Lingayen Gulf, Luzon, on 24th December 1941.** *Right:* **A subsidiary force lands on Mindanao one day later**

could have held out for quite some time. The assumption MacArthur continued to make, that the United States could send fresh supplies, was unrealistic. Once Japan controlled the seas and air, it would be suicidal for the United States to risk reinforcing Bataan when the Dutch East Indies were still holding out. When Singapore fell even this would have little effect. MacArthur later blamed Marshall for not having come through with the supplies he had promised. He asked Washington repeatedly for help but no help was forthcoming. MacArthur blamed the lack of a will-to-win in Washington for his defeat. This cannot be accepted as the real reason. Admiral Hart gave the Dutch East Indies higher priority than the Philippines; it had tin and rubber which was vital to Japanese as well as American interests, not to mention its oil. With limited supplies available to the Americans, priorities had to be made, no matter how valiant and futile the effort then being made in the Philippines seemed.

On 10th January MacArthur received a message from the Commander-in-Chief of the Japanese Expeditionary Force. Homma told MacArthur that he was 'well aware that you are doomed. The end is near. The question is how long you will be able to resist. You have already cut rations by half. I appreciate the fighting spirit of yourself and your troops who have been fighting with courage. Your prestige and honor have been upheld. However, in order to avoid needless bloodshed and to save the remnants of your divisions and your auxiliary troops, you are advised to surrender'. When MacArthur failed to answer this note, the Japanese showered Bataan with leaflets asking the soldiers to surrender despite what it called MacArthur's 'stupid refusal' to accept surrender proposals. Japan implored the Filipinos to surrender at once and 'build your new Philippines for and by Filipinos'. These attempts were falling on largely deaf ears mainly because of the Filipinos' faith in the Americans granting independence to them at an early date. The concept of a Philippine Commonwealth had paid off.

MacArthur refused to give up for two reasons. First, he was not the sort of man to surrender without a severe struggle. Second, he still expected the promised supplies to come from the States. Marshall undoubtedly made a mistake when he encouraged MacArthur's hopes, which did not have a prayer of being fulfilled. When President Roosevelt broadcast to the Philippine people on 28th December that the United States Navy 'is following an intensive and well-planned campaign against Japa-

The Japanese advance on Manila. *Left:*
Marines watch their mortars shelling
US positions. *Above:* Manila on fire
after Japanese bombing, 31st December

nese forces which will result in
positive assistance to the defense of
the Philippine Islands', he was leading
the Filipinos down the garden path.
They still had faith in MacArthur's
word and the word of President
Roosevelt, and the disillusionment
that followed was all the greater for
these assurances having been made.
However, it must be added that
MacArthur had begged Roosevelt to
give the Filipinos something to go
on, and the President's message was
largely inspired by MacArthur's insistence that some words of encourage-
ment ought to be made. Again, the
lack of political expertise on Mac-
Arthur's part was to injure his cause.
There wasn't a chance of MacArthur
receiving any aid. Brigadier-General
Eisenhower told Marshall as early as
10th December that it would be a long
time before any major reinforcements
could be sent to the Philippines and
that therefore America's major base
had to be Australia. Marshall agreed
with this assessment. Nothing was to
be gained by holding out false hopes
to MacArthur's forces on the Bataan
Peninsula.

Misinformation of another sort was
to further affect MacArthur's judgement of the situation. He believed that
Japan had six divisions in the Philippines, not two. By passing this misinformation on to Washington, it was
no wonder that the Americans had
given up the fight for the islands.
However, Homma was equally misin-
formed. He thought that the
Americans had only about 25,000 men
on Bataan, when they actually had
over three times that number. Homma
therefore assigned the siege of Bataan
to an inexperienced 65th Brigade and
a regiment from the 16th Division –
only nine battalions in all, plus
artillery and a tank regiment. The
invasion plan was to advance two

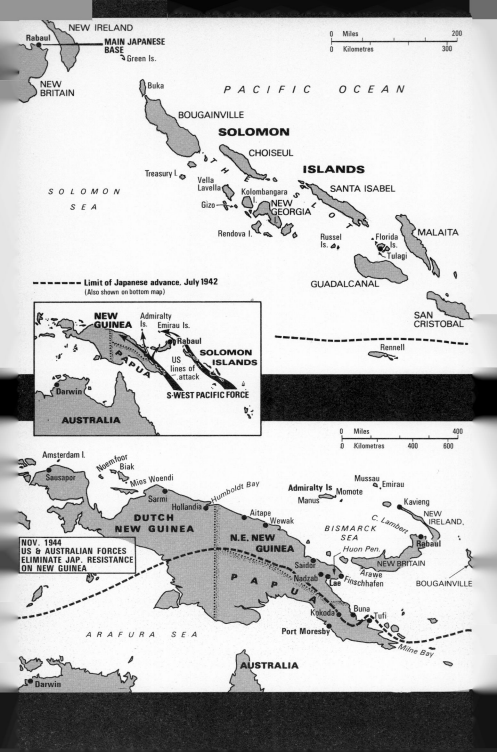

NEW IRELAND

Rabaul

MAIN JAPANESE BASE

Green Is.

NEW BRITAIN

PACIFIC OCEAN

Buka

BOUGAINVILLE

SOLOMON

CHOISEUL

ISLANDS

Treasury I.

Vella Lavella

Kolombangara I.

Gizo

NEW GEORGIA

SANTA ISABEL

MALAITA

SOLOMON SEA

Rendova I.

Russel Is.

Florida Is.

Tulagi

GUADALCANAL

SAN CRISTOBAL

------- Limit of Japanese advance, July 1942
(Also shown on bottom map)

NEW GUINEA

Admiralty Is.

Emirau Is.

Rabaul

SOLOMON ISLANDS

PAPUA

US lines of attack

Darwin

S-WEST PACIFIC FORCE

AUSTRALIA

Rennell

Amsterdam I.

Noemfoor

Biak

Sausapor

Mios Woendi

Sarmi

Hollandia

Humboldt Bay

DUTCH NEW GUINEA

Aitape

Wewak

Mussau

Emirau

Admiralty Is

Momote

Manus

Kavieng

NEW IRELAND.

C. Lambert

N.E. NEW GUINEA

BISMARCK SEA

Huon Pen.

Rabaul

NOV. 1944 US & AUSTRALIAN FORCES ELIMINATE JAP. RESISTANCE ON NEW GUINEA

NEW BRITAIN

Saidor

Arawe

Nadzab

Lae

Finschhafen

BOUGAINVILLE

PAPUA

Kokoda

Buna

Tufi

ARAFURA SEA

Port Moresby

Milne Bay

AUSTRALIA

Darwin

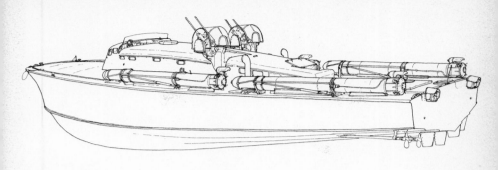

This is an American PT boat of the series numbered from 20 to 68. *Displacement:* 35 tons. *Dimensions:* 77 by 20 by 5½ feet. *Engines:* 3-shaft petrol engines, 4,050 hp, producing a speed of 40 knots. *Armament:* four 18-inch torpedo tubes and four Browning machine guns. *Crew:* 12

columns, one on either side of the peninsular.

By underestimating the Americans' strength, the Japanese were going to run into fierce and unexpected opposition. The attack, which began on 9th January, started off badly. When the Japanese were beaten back by a regiment of Philippine Scouts on the 11th, Major-General Akira Nara, in charge of the 65th Brigade, realized that he was going to face far stronger resistance than he expected, despite the attempts of 'Tokyo Rose' to weaken the Filipinos' and Americans' resolve through her nightly broadcasts to the troops. Brigadier-General George Parker, however, had been thrown back from the hills, and MacArthur's inland flank was exposed. On the 15th MacArthur sent another message to his troops, urging them to fight on because 'help is on the way from the United States. Thousands of troops and hundreds of planes are being dispatched . . . It is imperative that our troops hold until these reinforcements arrive. No further retreat is possible'. That MacArthur believed every word he said makes the situation even more tragic in retrospect.

Parker's men slowly withdrew after intense fighting while the Japanese carried out a similar maneuver in Wainwright's inland flank. By the 22nd MacArthur had ordered Sutherland to withdraw to a new line of defense. The Japanese had suffered heavy casualties in this sixteen-day battle, losing over 1,400 men, but were now faced with a shorter and stronger line, from Bagac to Orion, as the Americans repelled, with some difficulty, a seaborne attack on the southwest coast of the peninsula. The first Japanese thrusts against the Bagac-Orion line were repelled, and for a fortnight, despite heavy bombardment, the Japanese were unable to break through; at the same time the Japanese had been shelling Corregidor, where MacArthur kept his headquarters now, so much so that the original and rather exposed offices and quarters were abandoned for the safety of tunnels, where MacArthur's command was to continue its operations. Striding through the bunkers, smoking his corn-cob pipe, MacArthur

Above: 'Dugout Doug' MacArthur with General Sutherland in the bunker on Corregidor, 1st March 1942. Below: Japanese machine-gunners in the Bataan peninsula

presented a heroic and dashing figure to his men, dressed simply except for his walking stick and field-marshal's cap. Many of his men, especially those closest to him, were impressed by his *sang-froid* and calm demeanor in the face of disaster. This view, however, was not always shared by the men in the field, who called him 'Dugout Doug', since he had not emerged from Corregidor for weeks while the fierce fighting continued on Bataan. This unjust ballad was composed:

Dugout Doug MacArthur lies, a'shaking on the Rock

Safe from all the bombers and from any sudden shock.

This was hardly fair, since the Rock was under heavy and almost constant bombardment, and MacArthur sometimes went out of his tunnel-HQ to brave the hideous cacaphony and terror which destroyed everything standing above ground. MacArthur disdained wearing a protective helmet and was almost killed on more than one occasion when enemy shrapnel and bombs tore through the place where he was standing. As usual he was more than an example to his men when it came to personal heroism. But the frontline troops were unable to see their commander. He had recognized the importance of this in the First World War; but MacArthur was simply not the same man that he was then. More typical of the despair of those last weeks in Bataan was this refrain:

No mama, no papa, no Uncle Sam;

No aunts, no uncles, no cousins no nieces;

No pills, no planes, no artillery pieces.

. . . And nobody gives a damn.

Philippine morale, despite MacArthur's efforts, was flagging. General Aguinaldo, hero of the Spanish-American War, wrote MacArthur begging him to give up the fight in order to save lives which would be lost for nothing. MacArthur admitted being shaken by this message. On 8th February President Quezon sent a

President Manuel Quezon

message to Roosevelt through Marshall asking that the United States grant independence immediately to the Philippines, that the islands be neutralized, and that both American and Japanese forces be withdrawn. MacArthur sent an accompanying message, admitting that his men were exhausted and that 'complete destruction' might come at any time. Roosevelt replied that although he could not promise immediate aid, 'every ship at our disposal is bringing to the southwest Pacific the forces which will ultimately smash the invader' and MacArthur was urged to fight on to the end by FDR. The President added that if it were possible Quezon and his ministers should be flown to America via Australia. Quezon broadcast further appeals to his people and the fight went on, although Roosevelt authorized MacArthur to negotiate a capitulation if necessary. The timing would be left to MacArthur. MacArthur replied, 'I have not the slightest intention in the world of surrendering or capitulating the Filipino forces of my command. I intend to fight to destruction on Bataan and then do the same on Corregidor'. Marshall suggested that MacArthur's wife and

General Yamashita

young son be evacuated by submarine, and Quezon begged MacArthur to accept the offer. After conferring with his wife, MacArthur told Quezon, 'she will stay with me to the end. We drink from the same cup'. He told Marshall; 'I and my family will share the fate of the garrison'. Quezon, deeply moved, himself left soon after and slipped his signet ring on MacArthur's finger before he went with his family, telling him 'When they find your body, I want them to know you fought for my country'.

On 16th February MacArthur ordered yet another assault on the enemy forces. But on the 22nd, as the Japanese slowly pressed forward, MacArthur was ordered to go to Mindanao for not more than a week, after which he would be appointed to take command of all the Allied forces in the southwest Pacific with his headquarters in Australia. MacArthur later reported that his first reaction was simply to resign his commission and enlist as a soldier to stay with his men. On the 24th, persuaded by his staff officers that he should follow the directive, he replied that he would go but he would pick the right time in order to sustain flagging morale. He said that 15th March would probably be the right time. Homma's forces, however, had slackened their pressure on the peninsula, and on 9th March he was replaced by General Yamashita, who had just taken Singapore. The lull on Bataan had been going on now for three weeks and MacArthur decided that this was the right time to leave. Not waiting for the submarine, which was due to pick him up on the 15th, he and his family as well as some of his staff went to Mindanao in torpedo boats. They left Corregidor on 12th March and reached Mindanao on the 14th.

There was a good deal of scurrilous gossip floating around Corregidor that MacArthur had taken along phonographs, his collection of books and other personal items of value rather than taking more men with him, Mac-

General Wainwright (extreme left) surrenders to General Homma, Manila

Arthur denies this categorically. Yet there is still some evidence to support at least some of the gossip. Even if the story is completely without foundation, the fact that many of his men even now swear to the fact that the gossip is true is an indication of the sort of rapport MacArthur had with the majority of his men on the fortress island. Although most of those closest to him attest to his bravery in a crisis and his loyalty to his men, the majority of those in the field did not share this opinion. If MacArthur's motto had been to lead from the front in the First World War, his reputation was that of one who led from the rear and deserted in the face of the enemy when the chips were down at Bataan. Despite the fact that much if not all of this was unfair and untrue, inasmuch as the Commander-in-Chief, Roosevelt, ordered him to go to Australia, one cannot overlook the comments of many of who were to go to enemy prison camp for years as a result of the loss of the Philippines, and even the unfortunates who fell in the infamous March of Death to these camps after Corregidor fell. When Wainwright finally surrendered on 6th May, after a long and bitter fight that cost the enemy thousands of lives and the Americans and Filipinos thousands more, an estimated 140,000 men became prisoners of the Japanese throughout the archipelago.

The extravagant praise given MacArthur for his defense of the Philippines by members of his staff does not hold up under scrutiny. Despite the fact that money was scarce and materials for war were in short supply, MacArthur could still have done more to prepare the Philippines in the six years he had before the war broke out. The troops were painfully unready and MacArthur did not fully realize how unprepared they were. Although his errors on the morning of 8th December were not crucial to the loss of the Philippines, which probably would have been lost anyway, he should have realized that without sea and air superiority or even parity he had no chance of winning or preventing the Japanese from doing so. By continually promising his men and the Filipino public that help was coming, implying that this help would come imminently, MacArthur

Bataan surrenders. American troops
file out of their positions. The Japanese
are offering them cigarettes

betrayed the faith of those who believed in him.

While on Bataan and Corregidor his
failure to create a rapport with his
front-line troops did not help morale.
Even the long fight which the Japanese
had to endure to take the peninsula
cannot really be attributed to Mac-
Arthur's planning or strategy. The
fact that Homma was replaced in mid-
campaign and that the Japanese army
was weakened by the withdrawal of
their best troops to other areas
accounts more for the long delay in
the fall of Corregidor than any effort
of MacArthur's, although the valiance
of those who defended the peninsula
cannot be questioned. Although the
siege of Bataan cost the Japanese lives
and tied down some of their troops, it
tied down more American troops
and cost the Americans and Filipinos more. By the time MacArthur
reached Australia on the morning of
March 17th, the Battle of the Java Sea
had already been lost and the Dutch
East Indies had been taken by the Japanese. Southeast Asia was theirs and
the fighting on Bataan, for the Japanese anyway, was only a mopping-up
campaign. They could have taken
Bataan and Corregidor sooner if they
had not put first things first and placed
the Indies and Singapore as the top
priorities in the area.

Sir Edward Grey used to say, 'fine

words butter no parsnips'. All of Mac-Arthur's baroque prose during and after the event could not disguise the fact that the United States had suffered a crushing defeat in the Philippines and the Western Pacific. However, MacArthur's reputation at home in the States was enhanced by his noble phrases. Roosevelt found, to his surprise, that MacArthur emerged out of one of America's most stunning defeats as a hero in spite of himself; the fate of the beleaguered troops in Bataan touched a chord in the hearts of patriotic Americans, incensed by the surprise attack on Pearl Harbor and the heavy losses America and the Allies were suffering in the first months of 1942. Roosevelt, sensing this, saw that MacArthur's propaganda value was useful to the American war effort. When asked by reporters for a statement when he arrived in Australia, MacArthur, weary from the difficult journey, casually remarked, 'The President of the United States ordered me to break through the Japanese lines and proceed from Corregidor to Australia for the purpose, as I understand it, of organizing the American offensive against Japan, a primary object of which is the relief of the Philippines. I came through and I shall return'. This last phrase became a symbol of continued American resistance to Japan to both the Philippine and American public; MacArthur was awarded the Medal of Honor for his role in the Philippines.

The road back

After MacArthur arrived in Australia members of his staff flew to Melbourne, but MacArthur was met in Alice Springs in the interior of the country by Patrick J Hurley, who told him that every generation of Americans had its hero: Pershing, Dewey, Lindbergh; America, he said, had now taken MacArthur to their hearts as its hero. Music to MacArthur's ears, this praise was mitigated by the news MacArthur also received: there were only about 25,000 American troops in Australia and only 260 aircraft, many of them unusable. Panicky Australians suggested that the Allies withdraw to a Brisbane Line which would leave the whole of the north coast open to Japanese seizure. Although most reports that historians have at their disposal now indicate that the Japanese intended to consolidate their enormous gains and deal with Australia later, this was not known at the time. MacArthur was stunned by the news, and assured the Labour Prime Minister of Australia, John Curtin, that he would handle the front if Curtin took care of the rear. Curtin gave MacArthur unqualified support. MacArthur's receipt of the American Medal of Honor encouraged him and tended to put those rumours to rest which indicated that Marshall and MacArthur were not getting along. They were not, of course, and the situation was not made any better when, later in the year, MacArthur refused Marshall's suggestion that poor General Wainwright, then in captivity after the Death March, be granted the same honor.

MacArthur attended a meeting of the Advisory War Council in Canberra late in March, a body which was composed of members of the Australian ministry and members of the opposition, and told the body that he doubted whether Japan would press on to invade Australia right away. MacArthur assumed correctly that Japan was over-extended and

Allied Commander-in-Chief

Above: MacArthur is interviewed in Australia shortly after his escape from Corregidor. *Below:* General Sir Thomas Blamey

would only try to bomb northern Australian ports and perhaps to seize them but to go no further. He therefore rejected the idea of a Brisbane Line. He again insisted that the Allies concentrate on defeating Japan first rather than Germany, which as usual, ran counter to the accepted view and was not likely to gain a sympathetic ear in Washington, which, after all, was the ultimate authority for sending whatever supplies could be spared to the Pacific. MacArthur continued to harp on this theme throughout the rest of the war and therefore intensified the animosity felt toward him among many in high places in the United States. Such continued opposition on MacArthur's part was counterproductive and even less likely to yield the desired results than a policy of acquiescence, or, at least, sullen silence. Roosevelt was not wholly opposed to sending supplies to MacArthur's theatre of operations. Admiral King supported MacArthur's view in front of the President, but a policy of aiding Britain first remained the highest priority. At one stage Roosevelt was inclined to give MacArthur the 100,000 combat troops he asked for as well as the thousand planes, but he was finally persuaded that this was inadvisable, since it was generally felt that the buildup in Britain must not be slowed down whatever compelling reasons might be argued.

During the first few months in Australia MacArthur was a bitterly disappointed man. Not only had he just been defeated but the immediate prospects of making a return to the Philippines were dimming. Although the United States had begun an extraordinarily successful buildup of troops and material, by mid-1942 America was clearly not fully tooled up for war. American industry had stopped production of most consumer goods by this time, but retooling of factories and converting them into war plants was not and could not be an overnight

operation. MacArthur did not quite understand the problems of creating an army and a war machine within the United States and was, perhaps understandably, impatient at what he considered procrastinations and bureaucratic incompetence. While MacArthur was in the Philippines decisions had been made to send men to the Pacific theatre of operations, and many did go to India, Java and elsewhere. In fact, 57,000 got to Australia by mid-1942 and 79,000 were sent to the Pacific area as a whole, far more, in fact, than went to Britain and the European theatre of operations in the first months of that year. MacArthur had little to complain about considering the circumstances, but complain he did nevertheless.

A few days before he reached Australia the decision had been reached to re-organize the Allied commands which had already undergone several reorganization schemes already. There would be three main theatres of operations: the Pacific, directed by the American Joint Chiefs of Staff; Indian Ocean and Middle East, directed by the British Chiefs of Staff; and the European-Atlantic, under the joint responsibility of Britain and America. The Pacific

Prime Minister John Curtin

Vice-Admiral Herbert F Leary

theatre was divided into two main areas: Pacific Ocean, including the central, south and north Pacific areas; and the southwest Pacific, including Australia, New Guinea, the Philippines and most of the Indies. On 1st April MacArthur was ordered to hold the key military bases of Australia 'as bases for future offensive action'. Orders henceforth were to come through the American Joint Chiefs of Staff. On 18th April he assumed command of all Allied forces in the southwest Pacific and his immediate subordinates were announced. Of his senior staff, which was appointed the next day, only three members had not come' with MacArthur from the Philippines. Although urged by Marshall to do so, MacArthur resolutely refused to make room for Dutch and Australian officers to serve on his senior staff. Furthermore, most of his staff was drawn from the ranks of the US Army, rather than from all three services. His headquarters team was entirely drawn from the American Army, and the naval, land and air headquarters were housed separately. As a result MacArthur was not in close contact with air and naval experts. His immediate subordinates, General Sir

Thomas Blamey, Major-General George H Brett and Vice-Admiral Herbert F Leary, for example, did have representatives of all the Allies working under them, and therefore they created more the sort of command which MacArthur ought to have created on his own team. MacArthur, plagued by his feelings of isolation and neglect, had decided to draw around him his small and devoted staff, who had served him for so long and was not happy about diluting it with outsiders.

The naval and air forces at MacArthur's command at that time were meagre indeed: a few cruisers and submarines and a considerable number of smaller vessels of the Australian Navy. However, MacArthur was anxious to strike a counter-offensive at once. MacArthur's first directive relating to a general plan came on 25th April when he told the Allied land forces not to allow any Japanese landing on the northeast coast of Australia or the southwest coast of Australian-held New Guinea. This was short of an all-out offensive against New Guinea, but it was a positive step taken to ensure that the whole of the island did not fall into enemy hands.

By this time Corregidor had fallen and Port Moresby in New Guinea had been fortified with planes and a brigade of militia to support the small Papuan battalion. At Darwin, on Australia proper, a group of about 15,000 troops awaited the Japanese onslaught, although three US fighter squadrons were ready to help in the defense. It was at this point that the Japanese planned the next stage of their offensive: a seaborne expedition mounted at Rabaul and aimed at Port Moresby. The Americans, prepared for this offensive through the interception of decoded Japanese signals, concentrated a naval force in the Solomon Sea which included two carriers. Although the engagements on 5th-8th May cost the Allies the loss of the *Lexington*, an aircraft carrier,

Major-General George H Brett

as well as two other vessels, a small Japanese carrier was sunk and, more important, the Japanese were turned back. This stalemate was actually a victory inasmuch as the force in Port Moresby probably would not have been able to withstand concentrated Japanese pressure. By now there were only two undamaged American aircraft carriers in the Pacific and the Americans had reason to believe that Japan was about to mount an offensive against Hawaii.

On 12th May MacArthur told Curtin that the situation was bad and, furthermore, had already pressed Marshall for two carriers, three divisions and an increase in his air force. These continual messages were not going to change Washington's Hitler-first policy very much and served merely as an annoyance. There was little MacArthur could do at this stage except to send comforting messages to Wainwright until Corregidor fell and issue press releases which, admittedly, did much to sustain morale in the States. For example, he remarked that 'Corregidor needs no comment from me. It has sounded its own story at the mouth of its guns. It has scrolled its own epitaph on enemy tablets, but through the bloody haze of its last reverberating shots, I shall always seem to see the vision of its grim, gaunt and ghostly men, still unafraid'. But purple prose and onomatopoeia notwithstanding Wainwright was still not recommended for the Medal of Honor.

On 25th May MacArthur indicated that he expected a renewed attack on Port Moresby and therefore reinforced the town as well as sent troops to forward positions in Queensland. Soon afterwards, however, the great Japanese onslaught in the Central Pacific, long expected, took place, and in the Battle of Midway the Japanese carrier force suffered a stunning setback, the first major Allied victory of the war in the Pacific. Stirred by the victory MacArthur again implored Marshall for more men and weapons so as to capture the Japanese base at Rabaul and force the enemy back to his base on the island of Truk, 700 miles further north. He needed an amphibious division and at least two carriers plus a substantial naval force. There were serious objections to this plan. First of all, the carriers would be exposed to attack from enemy landbased aircraft, while at the same time Allied land-based aircraft could not protect the fleet. An army man to the fingernails, MacArthur still had a lot to learn about the importance of air power and the use of a navy. Marshall, however, was for the first time prepared to release major weapons to the Pacific as the American industrial machine and conscription had built up to the point where the Allies could afford to supply the Pacific theater as well.

By this time it was clear that there were to be two major commanders in the Pacific operating from two different directions in the attack on Japan. Admiral Chester W Nimitz was unhappy about the prospect of placing naval forces under the command of MacArthur, an army man, and therefore decided that he would launch his own operation from Hawaii westward while MacArthur, as commander in

the southwest Pacific, would push northwards toward the same objective. This did not mean, of course, that MacArthur would have no substantial naval force under his command; but it did mean that Nimitz and MacArthur would be competing against each other to see who could defeat Japan quicker. Roosevelt, always fond of this confrontation tactic in labor relations, within his own government and in the political arena, approved of this scheme. The natural rivalry between the Army and the Navy could be used to the advantage of the Allies, who, after all, were interested in defeating Japan regardless of who got the credit. The Navy hated MacArthur and the admirals welcomed this sort of confrontation. Stimson wrote that MacArthur was 'a constant bone of contention', and although his brilliance as a general was not always matched by his tact, 'the Navy's bitterness against him seemed childish'.

In any event by July a policy toward victory in the Pacific was finally decided by the Joint Chiefs of Staff. It was announced that the objective was to seize the New Britain-New Ireland-New Guinea area. This directive of 2nd July went on to say that a commander designated by Admiral Nimitz would take Santa Cruz, Tulagi (near Guadalcanal) and adjacent islands: MacArthur's forces would take the rest of the Solomons and the northeast coast of New Guinea, as well as Rabaul and adjacent positions in and around New Guinea and New Ireland. The island-hopping program had begun. MacArthur replied to this directive asking that the Tulagi-Santa Cruz operation be deferred in favor of the rest of the program, but Admiral King insisted on handling it according to the directive. MacArthur

The battle of the Coral Sea: the sinking of the *Lexington*. *Left:* Survivors climb aboard *USS Coral Sea*. *Below:* The *Lexington* on fire

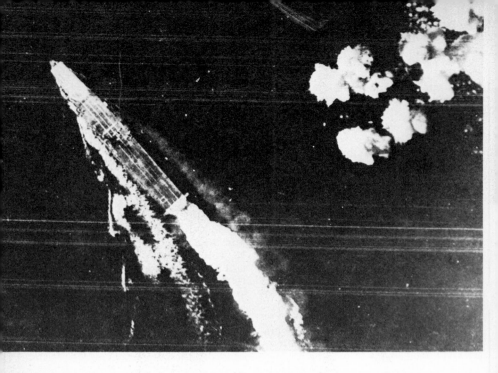

was correct in his second thoughts about the operation; he did not have the means to do all of this, but after having received messages from MacArthur for so long that he wanted to press ahead, King could see no reason why MacArthur had changed his mind all of a sudden.

MacArthur, it is true, was now confronting the realities and difficulties of the task he had before him. But the persistent lack of confidence MacArthur had in Washington and the Joint Chiefs, a feeling which he did not pretend to disguise, was counter-productive. He continued to argue that a second front in Europe was not realistic and that the best way to relieve the pressure on Russia was to launch a sustained attack on Japan with most of America's forces. These remarks not only made the situation vis à vis Washington worse; they were politically naïve in the extreme. Russia was not at war with Japan. What possible good

Above: The battle of Midway. The Japanese carrier *Hiryu* under attack
Right: Admiral Chester W Nimitz

would it do for Russia to have Japan defeated, except to eliminate a former and perhaps future enemy? Russia and America, for that matter, were obsessed with defeating Germany. With Russian troops pushed back a thousand miles or more into their own territory by the Germans, with America's European Allies, with one or two exceptions, already occupied by Germany, this was not an altogether unreasonable position to take.

Nevertheless, MacArthur took positive steps to fortify New Guinea and prepared to attack Rabaul. But the Japanese continued to press forward in New Guinea and Australian forces were slowly pushed back. On 25th August a second prong of the Japanese attack on Port Moresby began with a landing of some 2,000 marines near Milne Bay airstrip. The Australians

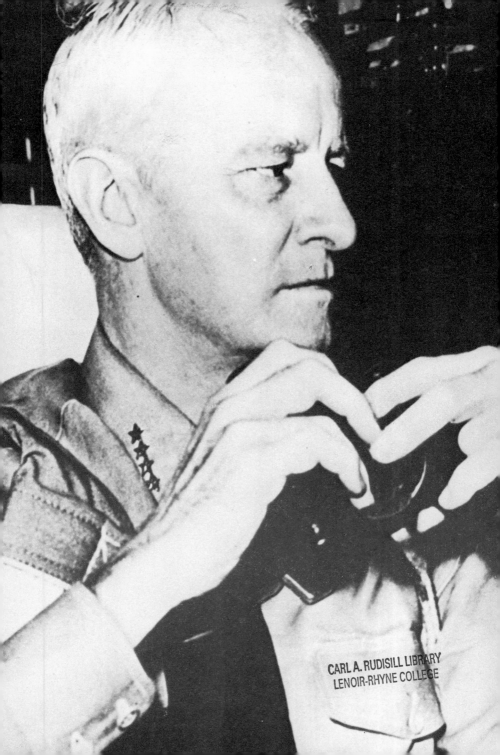

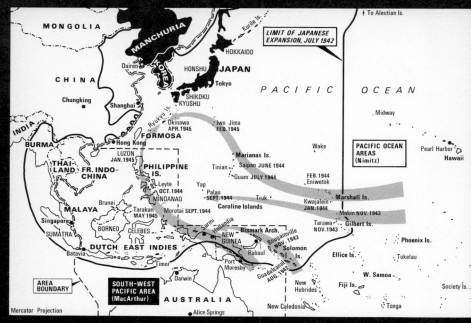

Progress of US forces

held back the advance after ten days of intense fighting and then began to push them back. This was the first defeat of a Japanese amphibious force in the war. MacArthur was understandably concerned about the Milne Bay operation, as well as the fact that the attack on Truk had resulted only in the Allies' attempting to hold on to their forward bases. MacArthur was unfamiliar with the problems of fighting in the mountains of East Asia and did not visit New Guinea personally until October. His optimism still was his greatest enemy. Invariably he would have to revise his over-estimation of Allied capabilities after having suffered setbacks. Part of the problem was that he was not fully informed. This was partly his own fault. His commanding, even forbidding, appearance which he actively cultivated made it difficult for him to have good working relationships with many of his subordinates. Major-General George Brett, his air commander, came under heavy criticism from MacArthur, and Brett knew that he was not liked by MacArthur. Therefore Brett had only been able to see MacArthur eight times in four months. When Brett was replaced by General George C Kenney, Kenney made it a point to be in and out of MacArthur's office, and an affection grew between the men which was to aid the Allied cause. Kenney's breezy ebullience cheered up MacArthur, who was still depressed from the defeat in the Philippines.

From the time Kenney came to MacArthur the General's relationship with his other subordinates softened somewhat, therefore bringing him into closer contact which would permit him to be closer to current information and intelligence than he previously had been. Personal loyalty to MacArthur was the key variable: without it and without stating it often to the General, one was kept from the inner circle and one was eventually faced with MacArthur's wrath. The court-like atmosphere so evident in Manila was sustained in Australia, albeit with some modifications.

The first phase of the Joint Chiefs' offensive began on 8th August when the First Marine Division had been put ashore at Tulagi and Guadalcanal; beginning the long war of attrition and island-hopping. Although the Americans lost a carrier and two others had been damaged, heavy casualties had been suffered by the Japanese, and by September 20,000 Allied soldiers were ashore. At the same time MacArthur carefully launched an offensive against the Japanese in New Guinea. MacArthur pressed Nimitz for more material, and Nimitz told him that he could spare nothing more. MacArthur then used this as an excuse for not throwing heavy land forces into New Guinea. MacArthur would have to make the best of what he had, and he did. MacArthur was dissatisfied with the way the Australians had been unable to completely dislodge the Japanese from Milne Bay and told both Marshall and Curtin that he intended to send in American troops to reinforce them, which he considered far superior to the Australian soldiers. While all this controversy was going on behind the scenes, the Japanese had ordered a withdrawal, as they had run out of supplies and could not sustain their offensive.

Argument faded in the light of the Japanese decision as the Allied troops pushed forward. The campaign in New Guinea had failed thus far because MacArthur had laid greater emphasis on taking Guadalcanal than on clearing Papua. This was a correct decision. If the Solomons could be taken the Japanese in New Guinea would be cut off and could be defeated more easily. Once men and supplies had been slowly built up MacArthur was prepared to make an all-out offensive in New Guinea. On 1st October the orders were issued for an Allied advance along two lines of attack, while other forces cleared the Milne Bay area. But MacArthur still

Left: MacArthur takes tea with Australian troops in New Guinea, May 1942. *Above:* With Blamey at Port Moresby, November 1942

emphasized taking Guadalcanal above the New Guinea offensive. Both Roosevelt and MacArthur had misgivings about the delay in taking the island and MacArthur went so far as to suggest on 31st October that if things became worse on Guadalcanal he was prepared to withdraw from the Allied-held section of the north coast of Papua in order to reinforce Guadalcanal. But air drops to the men in the Owen Stanley Range worked, even though maneuverability through the mountains was extremely difficult. The pincer movement heading toward Buna was now beginning to achieve results by November, at the same time as the Japanese suffered heavy losses in their defense of Guadalcanal. The Allies were unaware that the Japanese supplies and men were exhausted and by now they were facing an outnumbered enemy force which was holding on in much the same way as the beleaguered Americans had held on for so long in Bataan and Corregidor.

The Buna beachhead on the north coast of Papua was not easy to take, much to MacArthur's concern. Two weeks of fighting in November and a four-pronged Allied offensive had been stopped dead. Malaria and dysentery affected the Americans and the Japanese defenses were tough to crack. Allied supplies were still not plentiful and since the emphasis was still on Guadalcanal, few supplies reached the Allied forces surrounding Buna. MacArthur was now under criticism, since his Americans had been unable to capture the fortress and he was convinced that they had shown cowardice in the face of the enemy on New Guinea. He decided to send General Robert Eichelberger out there to sort out the difficulty and told him before he left to take Buna 'or don't come back alive'. Eichelberger was appalled at the situation near Buna. The condition of the troops was

Above left: MacArthur and General
George Kenney, January 1943. Kenney's
arrival transformed MacArthur's
public personality. *Below left:* US
Marines clear a Japanese dugout, New
Guinea, January 1943. *Above:*
Eichelberger

terrible and he agreed with MacArthur
that the men lacked 'inspired leadership'. He replaced the commander in
charge, Harding, with Major-General
Waldron, but realized that without
reinforcements it would be impossible
to take Buna. A fresh Australian
brigade was sent but it was not until
2nd January 1943 that Buna was
finally taken.

Even though MacArthur was in-
sensed at Australian criticism of his
own American troops, he knew that
there was an element of truth in their
criticisms. Knowing that he would
receive no reinforcements until after
Guadalcanal had been taken, he had
already pressed the Australians to
return some of their combat troops
from the Middle East, which, understandably enough, was not done,
since these troops were engaged at
El Alamein at the time. Despite all

hese difficulties, however, the last apanese stronghold at Buna was aken on 22nd January. Of the estimated 20,000 Japanese soldiers who anded on New Guinea, about 13,000 vere killed. But Allied losses were ormidable. There were over 3,000 Allied dead, and 28,000 more were suffering from malaria. The cost in ives was greater in Papua for the Allies than on Guadalcanal, where oughly 1,600 American lives were ost. The clean-up campaign on Papua was difficult as well, although on 4th January it is now known that Japan made the decision to abandon both Papua and Guadalcanal. Kenney's supply aircraft prevented Japan from sending in further supplies to their beleaguered troops in southern New nea. The real variable which had ged was control of the sea and the which by the end of 1942 had passed the hands of the Allies. The Southwest Pacific was open for reconquest, and MacArthur was right to have emphasized going on the offensive when his supplies had built up to the point of superiority over the weary Japanese.

MacArthur, however, despite the fact that he now knew he was winning, was still issuing communiques which greatly exaggerated Allied gains. These were designed to encourage morale at home, but have distorted the historical record. Often the reports would indicate that Allied troops had captured such-and-such an area, and this would give Americans in the States the impression that the effort probably was largely if not wholly American. Many reporters were later surprised to discover an area in Australian hands when they expected that the area had been taken by the Americans. MacArthur's distrust of Washington may have been one of his motives for issuing distorted and sometimes false communiques. But MacArthur's in-

ordinate desire for publicity and praise was probably the chief reason. The American public became convinced that the turning of the tide in the Pacific, which actually took place at the Battle of Midway, in which MacArthur played no part, was because of MacArthur's stunning victories and his military genius. It would be futile to denigrate MacArthur as a general; as a military man, although he made mistakes, he had few equals. But he wanted more than victory: he wanted glory.

Through these communiques as well as through his real achievements MacArthur had become a hero to the American public. Senator Vandenberg of Michigan suggested that he be nominated on the Republican ticket at the presidential elections to take place in 1944, a prospect which MacArthur would have dearly loved. A long-time student of the Civil War, MacArthur would have seen the parallel with McClellan, the Union general who did not get along with his President, and who ran against his former commander-in-chief in the elections of 1864. Roosevelt would have seen the parallel too; McClellan ran against President Lincoln.

All this is not to imply that MacArthur did not deserve what praise he did receive; after the battle in the Bismarck Sea MacArthur was awarded the Distinguished Service Medal for the third time from his President and the British gave him the Grand Cross of the Order of the Bath. MacArthur's first year as Allied Commander-in-Chief ended with decisive success in the three main areas of attack despite the frustrations of the early days: Milne Bay, central Papua and southern New Guinea. Although MacArthur made the broad plans and the men did the fighting, as is usual, MacArthur took the credit, which did not entirely endear him to his troops but which had extraordinary success in building his reputation as a military genius in the United States.

MacArthur's popular fame made some consider him for the Presidency

Advance to the Philippines

By the spring of 1943 the tide of victory had decisively turned in favor of the Allies. Germany had been repelled at Stalingrad, the Allies had begun their long march across the desert in North Africa after the victory at El Alamein and were preparing to clear North Africa in their attempt to invade Italy from the south. Soon Italy would have left the war.

In the Pacific the results did not appear as decisive as in Russia and the Mediterranean. Although Japan had abandoned Guadalcanal and they were on the run in New Guinea, MacArthur still felt that he had been denied the material which he required to follow up the Japanese retreat with solid victories. Many of his units were tired, although the Seventh Fleet and Admiral 'Bull' Halsey's naval forces as well as the 13th Air Force and Kenney's 5th Air Force had now become formidable weapons. MacArthur now realized that his decision to maintain a separate air arm was a mistake and ad-

mitted this to Kenney, who had done so well in co-ordinating combined ground and air offensives. All this did not alter the Allies' long-term plans to continue with the assumption that Hitler was the main enemy, and that MacArthur and his colleagues should conduct primarily a holding operation in the Pacific until the war had been conclusively won by the Allies in Europe. About thirty per cent of America's fighting strength was in the Pacific, and General Marshall intended to keep it that way. However, Roosevelt did agree that if an invasion of France did not take place in 1943, he would send more supplies to the Pacific. The planning was to take Rabaul, secure the Aleutians and advance on Truk and the Marianas via the Marshalls and the Gilberts. Operations in the Pacific would be placed last along with the C-B-I (China-Burma-India) theater in the list of

The War Lord. MacArthur watches a naval bombardment, 1944

priorities. Furthermore, the American
Navy was determined to make the
victory in the Pacific a largely Navy
affair.

MacArthur thought it incredible
that the Navy should take so nar-
row a view and allow inter-service
rivalry to determine the course of the
war. Through the insistence of Admiral
King, MacArthur's and Nimitz's commands remained separate, despite
MacArthur's urging and Washington's
realization of the fact that this was
not the most practical scheme.
MacArthur was not the only egotist
in the American military hierarchy,
and King was as determined as
MacArthur was to gain most of the
glory for himself and for the Navy.
The trouble was that King was not as
good a publicist of himself as
MacArthur.

In order to sort out the confusion
a meeting was called among representatives of the Southwest Pacific
command, South Pacific and Central
Pacific areas in mid-March, 1943.
MacArthur's representative, Sutherland, presented a plan code-named
Elkton. The estimates showed that
between 79,000 and 94,000 Japanese
still remained in northern New Guinea
and the Solomons with 383 aircraft,
four battleships, two aircraft carriers
and four cruisers. Reinforcements
could be sent to them. The *Elkton*
plan proposed a five-stage program:
seizure of airfields on the Huon Peninsula to support landings on New
Britain; seizure of airfields on New
Georgia; seizure of airfields on New
Britain and Bougainville; capture of
Kavieng, isolating Rabaul; and finally,
capture of Rabaul. Halsey and
MacArthur demanded five more divisions to accomplish this task, plus
forty-five more air groups as well as
additional naval forces. Sutherland
had to tell MacArthur almost upon
arrival at the meeting that these

would not be forthcoming. After interminable discussions it was decided to accept a plan similar to *Elkton*, but that the operations in the Solomons would be conducted by Halsey, under the general supervision of MacArthur. Halsey went to Brisbane to discuss *Elkton* with MacArthur. The two men impressed each other enormously. MacArthur reported, 'I liked him from the moment we met'. Halsey felt the same, and at the time persuaded MacArthur to attack New Georgia at once, and some of the requirements MacArthur called for were met.

Admiral King was anxious for action to get under way since there had been continuing operations in New Guinea. After the conference called Trident was held in Washington in May, it was decided that a two-pronged offensive be launched against Japan in the Pacific and that MacArthur would get seven more divisions which he needed to carry out *Elkton*. The Joint Chiefs told MacArthur that they wanted to

Right: The parachute drop at Nadzab, New Guinea, to cut off the Japanese retreat from Lae. *Above:* MacArthur with his B-17 crew after the drop

open an offensive against the Marshalls and asked him for a timetable. He suggested that the Allies move on a south-to-north axis, moving through New Guinea to Mindanao. He was still obsessed with getting to the Philippines as quickly as possible. He told the Joint Chiefs that the withdrawal of two marine divisions out of his theater would make the capture of Rabaul impossible. Finally an agreement was reached whereby he would take the northeast New Guinea coast by 1st September and attack New Britain on 1st December or thereabouts. Marshall also tried to take two bomber groups away from MacArthur's command but was unsuccessful this time. One might well ask why MacArthur always seemed starved of troops and weapons, and the answer is simple enough: priori-

Once MacArthur was placed in Australia in charge of operations in the Southwest Pacific he also had to accept a less active part in the early stages of the war. Hawaii, after all, was closer to Japan and the object of the war was to defeat and eventually occupy Japan, not the Philippines. With the Pacific theater low in priority in comparison with the Mediterranean, the Atlantic and the North Sea, MacArthur stood low in the priorital totem pole. However much noise emanated from his head-quarters nothing could alter that. But MacArthur was driven, not only to prove himself and to avenge Bataan, but to protect his men and supply them properly, which is the object and duty of any concientious commander. It was not the fact that MacArthur pushed for more troops and equip-ment; it was the way he did it.

Tarawa, Gilbert Islands, November 1943
Above: Marines storm Japanese positions on the devastated island
Right: After the costly action

By the end of June the south end of New Georgia had been taken by Halsey's men, and for several months the struggle in the Solomons con-tinued with heavy loss of life, equal at that point only to Buna and Guadal-canal. It was not until early October that the Solomons were secured, and their fighters were now operating over Bougainville, the next stepping-stone to Rabaul. Kenney's air force was building up gradually while, at the same time, the Japanese were re-sisting the army on New Guinea less and less as the Allies slowly pushed forward. MacArthur was surprised by being awarded the Air Medal for the airborne and parachute attack by the 503rd Parachute Regiment on Nadzab in New Guinea in September. The New Guinea campaign picked up steam and after Lae was taken on 11th

September, MacArthur decided upon a plan of amphibious landings behind enemy lines which was to become the hallmark of his operations in the Pacific. An advance on Finschhafen was ordered, and it was taken on 2nd October. It was proposed by Marshall that similar tactics should be used to isolate Rabaul, which MacArthur claimed was essential for his naval base to support further operations. As it turned out, Rabaul was not taken and was not nearly as necessary to MacArthur's plans as he had thought. But as the Allies advanced, new plans were being made.

In August MacArthur sent his outline plan, code-named *Reno*, to take the Philippines. After he had taken Rabaul (its possession was assumed) he would move along western New Guinea and thence to Mindanao via the Celebes. He claimed he could not reach Mindanao before 1945, perhaps later. The joint planners in Washington, however, assumed that MacArthur would either take or neutralize Rabaul by 1st February, 1944, and would get to Hollandia in Dutch New Guinea no later than 1st August of that year. They insisted that MacArthur bypass Rabaul, despite MacArthur's insistence that he had to take it. They also stressed the point that Nimitz's operations in the central Pacific would take priority over MacArthur's, and they pointed out that Nimitz would be closer to the Philippines according to their plans than MacArthur would when its forward movement reached Palau. The overall plan was to take the Philippines in 1945 and 1946 along with Formosa, the Ryukyus and Malaya. Japan would not be invaded until 1947 and would not be conquered until 1948. At the Quadrant conference in Quebec in August 1943 the British questioned the wisdom of advancing towards Japan on two

In Australia, 1943

axes and suggested that MacArthur merely hold his gains while Nimitz made the main drive across the Central Pacific. This would allow more men and material to be requisitioned for the invasion of Europe in 1944. This time Marshall and King came to MacArthur's aid and insisted on carrying their plans forward as scheduled. However, Quadrant offered MacArthur no new troops for his forces and no coherent program.

At this point MacArthur offered the Joint Chiefs a revised *Reno* plan which proposed a compromise on Rabaul: it would first be bypassed but captured later on. Rabaul would be isolated by 1st February and after operations on New Guinea, Mindanao would be attacked in February 1945. Despite Sutherland's efforts on MacArthur's behalf in Washington, it was decided that no new forces could be spared for MacArthur's plan. As a matter of fact, it is interesting to note that the policy of attrition towards the Joint Chiefs which MacArthur was waging was, to some extent, working. Thirteen American Army divisions were now in the Pacific employed against Japan compared with the same number employed against Germany. Although seventy-five groups of the Army Air Force were in the European Theatre of Operations as compared with thirty-five in the Pacific, the heavy concentration of naval power in the Pacific at this time more than offset this number.

Furthermore Halsey was moving faster than he had expected against increased Japanese resistance. As the bombing of Rabaul was stepped up by Kenney, New Zealanders occupied the Treasuries. MacArthur decided to place some of his forces across the Japanese line of withdrawal after Finschhafen fell and a landing was made at Saidor on 2nd January, 1944. By the time the Japanese retreat across northern New Guinea ended in March 1944 with the Japanese back at Wewak, only 54,000 remained of the Japanese army of 90,000 or so which began the fighting in September. MacArthur now could see the way clear to return to the Philippines, his dream and preoccupation since he left Corregidor, with control of the sea lanes and the air largely in his hands. Meanwhile, the central Pacific campaign was gathering momentum, with Tarawa and the Gilberts taken in November, 1948, and Nimitz was ordered to make a full-scale carrier attack on Truk. Nimitz and MacArthur would race for the Philippines after all, and with Nimitz's operations having priority from Washington, MacArthur could not expect to get further major shipments of supplies and men until after April, 1944, as Nimitz was expected to attack the western Marshalls after having taken Truk, or, failing that, to seize the Palaus. They would be the launching pad for an attack on Philippines, by by-passing Truk.

This was not entirely to MacArthur's liking. If anyone was to take the Philippines it would be him. Conspiracy theories, as usual, abounded in MacArthur's headquarters. Various groups were blamed for MacArthur's relegation to a back seat in the drive across the Pacific. At one time perfidy in the State

In February 1944 MacArthur accompanied the invasion forces to Los Negros in the Admiralty Islands. *Below:* With Admiral Kinkaid during the bombardment. *Above:* MacArthur and an aide pose ashore

Left: US Marines wade ashore at Aitape, North-East New Guinea, 22nd April 1944
Above: On the same day another landing is made at Hollandia, Dutch New Guinea
Below: MacArthur visits his men at Hollandia

Above: 14th September 1944 US troops land at Morotai, in the Molucca Islands, and gain control of the island in forty-eight hours. *Below:* MacArthur goes ashore on the first day, and tours the bridgehead, before returning to New Guinea (right)

Department, another time the Joint Chiefs, Roosevelt himself: all were charged with collusion with one sinister group after another; British imperialists, Communists: it had to have been someone's fault. Many innuendos crept into the frequent press conferences given by MacArthur; stage settings in which MacArthur could give a virtuoso performance before the dazzled eyes of the world, claiming victory, lack of support from the States and the brilliance of his own generalship. Reporters often were not taken in by the spectacular one-man shows, but enough of the aura of infallibility permeated the atmosphere so that the story could be transmitted to the States. As a result, a calculated effort on MacArthur's part, combined with an absolutely sincere belief that unpatriotic forces were at work within the States which hoped to deny him his triumphs, created an atmosphere of public opinion highly favorable to MacArthur.

It cannot be forgotten that most American newspapers, especially those in the West and Midwest, were owned by arch-Republican interests who resented Roosevelt's treble (it was to be quadruple) victory over the Republicans in the presidential elections since 1932. Many of their reporters knew it to be good for their own interests on the newspapers if an inordinate amount of glory were heaped on the shoulders of a general with arch-Republican sympathies while, at the same time, denigrating the role of the Democratic commander-in-chief, implying that he could have done more to win the war and bring the boys home quicker. MacArthur was in touch with Republican interests in the States. His political campaign was aimed over the heads of those in Washington on the Joint Chiefs and in the State Department and the White House who were opposed to what MacArthur was doing for legitimate reasons of their own. Failing to succeed politically with his superiors, MacArthur hoped to succeed at the ultimate power base, the people. In any event Sutherland was sent to Pearl Harbor to confer with the representatives of

the three Pacific command areas on MacArthur's behalf, at the end of January 1944.

The conference agreed that the Marianas were too far away from Japan to effectively use the B-29 bombers, and that therefore Japan would have to be attacked from bases in China. In this event Truk could be bypassed by Nimitz after all and the attack carried directly to the Palaus. MacArthur obviously was upset by this decision and urged the Joint Chiefs in February that if he were given more forces (again the same tired, repetitive note appears) he could be in the Philippines by the end of the year. He again suggested a huge force to be concentrated along the New Guinea-Mindanao axis in order to push northward at a fairly rapid speed. By this time his plans were quite unrealistic. It would have been impossible for Admiral King to justify slowing down the already successful Central Pacific advance, even though MacArthur had achieved far more in

his area. While Nimitz had repelled the Japanese advance on Hawaii and managed to seize islands on the perimeter of Japan's defensive arc, MacArthur had taken most of northern New Guinea, and successfully defended southern New Guinea, and had gone on to take the Solomons and had advanced to New Britain. It may have been possible that the Joint Chiefs had begun to believe a bit of MacArthur's propaganda themselves. However grandiose his claims may have been, MacArthur had done an excellent job so far; or at least since he left Bataan.

The Joint Chiefs and the conference at Pearl Harbor insisted that MacArthur carry on with the bombing of Rabaul and that the strongly defended enemy base of Kavieng be taken rather than bypassed as Halsey suggested. Kenney believed that Manus 'was the most important piece of real estate' in the area and if that could be taken, the whole of the Bismarck Sea would be in Allied

competed with each other in terms of victories over the Japanese, the end of the war could only come that much sooner. Formosa was made Nimitz's ultimate objective, and he was told to plan to be there by February 1945; MacArthur's, Luzon.

With Rabaul isolated and the Japanese forces in New Guinea neutralized and on the run, MacArthur was confident that he could make his way towards the Philippines with his naval support and air superiority. By April Hollandia was taken at a cost of little over 600 men, bypassing the 50,000-strong force at Wewak. As the allies made their successful landing in Normandy, which made certain that the war in Europe would soon come to an end, MacArthur seized Biak, in July Noemfoor fell, and in September, Morotai. All of New Guinea was now in Allied hands and MacArthur was island-hopping towards the Philippines, all at a cost of very few lives. At the same time Nimitz advanced to the Marianas and Palaus, closer to the Ryukyus than MacArthur's forces. The Ryukyus were the last stage in the island hopping which was to end with Japan itself. At an enormous cost in lives Saipan had been taken, and in July Guam was recaptured at a cost of almost 1,500 American lives. The Palaus were also a costly victory for Nimitz. Thus, in Europe, where the Allies had stressed the importance of a single united drive toward Germany under Eisenhower's leadership, this sort of plan was made impossible because of the mutual jealousy of the army and navy in the Pacific. By September MacArthur moved his headquarters to Hollandia from Brisbane, and the final drive for the Philippines was to begin.

Despite heavy American losses at Bougainville, MacArthur's race to the Philippines seemed to have been won. Both Nimitz and MacArthur were asked if they could step up their timetable for victory, and each said that they could not unless they were given more power. The Joint Chiefs were determined to hasten the end of the war by taking Japan, and were not as concerned as Nimitz and MacArthur seemed to be which areas before Japan were to be taken first. MacArthur urged the Joint Chiefs that the idea of bypassing the whole of the Philippines in favor of a final thrust toward Japan was politically unwise. Marshall felt that 'personal and political considerations' should not interfere with the main task at hand. He was convinced that if Formosa and the Ryukyus were taken this would help the final liberation of the Philippines, although this would mean that, like Rabaul, they would be taken at the end of the war. Looking at the situation cooly in the summer of 1944, it was not in fact necessary for the Allies to take the Philippines in order to win the war against Japan, just as it was not absolutely vital for China, the Dutch East Indies, Singapore, Indo-China or any other part of Southeast Asia to fall into Allied hands if the ultimate objective was the occupation and capitulation of Japan.

As had been argued so eloquently in Europe (by Stalin, among others), the way to defeat Germany was not to attack Italy, but it was to attack Germany as quickly and as directly as possible. So it was with respect to Japan. But there was more at stake than victory, according to MacArthur. He did not want to break faith with his abandoned and imprisoned troops in the Philippines; he did not want to break faith with the Filipinos; to him, and to his sense of honor, once the Philippines had been recaptured he had played his part in the war. The capture of Japan itself would be a glorious epilogue to his odyssey. A conference had to be called to settle these differences, of which Roosevelt was more than aware, and Nimitz and MacArthur were invited to meet the Commander-in-Chief on 26th July in Pearl Harbor. The question was not if the war was to be won, but when and how.

The warrior returns

MacArthur had already proposed several plans for his role in the conclusion of the war. He claimed that he could be in Mindanao by 25th October, Leyte on 15th November and with the help of six divisions, Luzon by April 1945. The controversy between the army and the navy required that these points be settled at once. Tojo had resigned on 18th July, and in Japan itself, although the military was still in control of the government, as it had been since late 1941, if not in many respects earlier, inter-service rivalry had divided the military to a much greater extent than it had done among the Americans in the Pacific. A plan was afoot in Japan to make a compromise peace with the intercession of Russia, which was still neutral in the Pacific war, but little came of it. As is usual in history, the conclusion of the war and the making of a peace is far more complex a problem than fighting it, and Roosevelt, on the threshold of victory in both Europe and Asia, was anxious to have a confrontation of all the major parties involved before the final push was made; because the final push would determine the nature of the peace.

MacArthur was not certain that President Roosevelt would attend the meeting in Hawaii, but he was 'reasonably certain that he would be there'. Since MacArthur was invited personally and had never attended any of the big staff conferences (and as he later remarked, never was invited again), he assumed that something important was to be decided. Neither Marshall nor Admiral King were there, however, and since Roosevelt had just been nominated for a fourth term by the Democratic Party, it was felt in some circles that Roosevelt merely wanted to underline his role as Commander-in-Chief for the forthcoming elections in November 1944. Despite these criticisms, there seems little doubt that a conference at that

An idealised portrait of MacArthur distributed in 1944

time was not merely a political exercise, and MacArthur felt the same. He came with no staff officers other than personal ADCs, and he was a bit surprised to see that Nimitz had come prepared with assistants, maps and all the paraphernalia which usually accompanies conferences on a high level. Nimitz was surprised himself that MacArthur had not come as well equipped as he was, and when the conference opened on 28th July MacArthur was asked by Nimitz if he had been told what the subject of the conference was to be about; MacArthur replied that he had not. MacArthur later reported that Nimitz 'seemed amazed and somewhat shocked.' MacArthur felt that he was going to have to 'go it alone'.

Nimitz first presented a plan, which MacArthur felt certain was really King's, of bypassing the Philippines, and that all American forces in the Southwest Pacific area were to be transferred to Nimitz's direct command, save two divisions. The advance was proposed to continue through the Central Pacific and the Allies would invade Formosa in early 1945. MacArthur again opposed this scheme both on military and political grounds. He argued that possession of the Philippines would prevent supplies from reaching Japan from the south and force her to an early capitulation because she would be starved of vital resources. He felt that frontal attacks on Iwo Jima and Okinawa would be unduly costly, as many of Nimitz's earlier triumphs had been, and that the Philippines, with its largely pro-Allied population, would be a better base from which to launch attacks on Japan than Formosa, with its largely hostile population. Roosevelt argued that a frontal attack on the Philippines would be even more costly. MacArthur argued that the United States had a moral obligation to free the Philippines as soon as possible. He argued that 'to bypass isolated islands

Admiral Nimitz on Guam, 1944

was one thing, but to leave in your rear such a large enemy concentration as the Philippines involved serious and unnecessary risks'. MacArthur replied to Roosevelt's argument that the cost in Allied lives would be too dear by saying, 'Mr. President, my losses would not be heavy, anymore than they have been in the past. The days of frontal attack should be over. Modern infantry weapons are too deadly, and frontal assault is only for mediocre commanders. Good commanders do not turn in heavy losses.' With this riposte out of the way, MacArthur went on to explain his plan, which would include a reconquest of the Dutch East Indies by the First Australian Army after the Philippines had been taken. Admiral Leahy accepted his ideas and in the end, so did Roosevelt, who apparently, according to MacArthur, was 'physically just a shell of the man I had known. It was clearly evident that his days were numbered.'

Roosevelt later asked MacArthur what he thought of the forthcoming election when they were inspecting troops together. MacArthur guardedly answered that he knew nothing of the political situation at home and denied that he would accept the nomination as the Republican candidate for President, a denial which Roosevelt doubted. Roosevelt had been worried for some months that MacArthur might accept the blandishments offered to him by some Republicans; MacArthur would have made a formidable candidate at that time; the war hero returned. When the Australian Prime Minister Curtin had told Roosevelt some time earlier that he was certain that MacArthur wanted to retain his command. Roosevelt was 'obviously delighted.' Curtin later told MacArthur that 'every night when he turned in, the President had been looking under the bed to make dead sure that you weren't there.' The meeting with Roosevelt created renewed confidence of both men in each other.

MacArthur, Roosevelt, and Nimitz meet at Pearl Harbor, 26th July 1944

The issue about a Philippine invasion was not finally settled until the Joint Chiefs met in September and agreed with MacArthur's proposal to attack Leyte on 20th December. Halsey's planes had attacked Mindanao and the Visayas and had reported that the areas were 'wide open', while reports trickling in from the Philippines indicated that there were no Japanese on Leyte. Nimitz put forward the proposal that since that was the case, Mindanao should be bypassed and Leyte be attacked at once. At this point MacArthur was on his way to Morotai, but Sutherland replied to Marshall's inquiry that the reports that there were no Japanese on Leyte were incorrect. MacArthur's contacts with the Philippines were excellent and better than Nimitz's or Washington's, since he was in touch with a guerrilla network operating in the archipelago. He was certain that at least 20,000 Japanese were on Leyte and that reinforcements could easily be deployed to the island. The Joint Chiefs decided that MacArthur should be lent escort carriers and other vessels from Nimitz's command in the Palaus for the assault on Leyte.

MacArthur's plan called for a commando battalion to assault the entrance to Leyte Gulf on 17th October, and that the first waves would go ashore on the 20th. Halsey's Third Fleet would provide naval protection and Kenney's air forces plus the Australian RAAF Command would give close support and air cover. The fact that about 174,000 troops were available for this operation made it the largest yet undertaken in the Pacific. MacArthur still had to retain large numbers of troops behind the lines as so many Japanese troops had been bypassed already that sufficient numbers of Allied forces had to be maintained for mopping up operations as well as for the defense of already-held bases in Bougainville,

New Britain and Australian New Guinea. In any event with British approval, as Churchill was beginning to take a greater interest in MacArthur and the Pacific war now that the European war was entering its final stages, further Australian and American reinforcements were sent to MacArthur's command. Finally MacArthur was getting all the support he needed. A newly-formed American Eighth Army under Eichelberger was sent to relieve Krueger's remaining tasks of the Sixth Army in New Guinea and Morotai. In mid-October Kenney's and Halsey's aircraft struck at Japanese airfields throughout Formosa and the Philippines. The Japanese were convinced that they had repelled Halsey's ships, when in fact they had not sunk even one. But reports to the contrary convinced Japan that it would be worth while to mobilize a huge naval force to defend the Philippines as well as a tired but still effective air force. MacArthur was convinced that Leyte would be the decisive battle of the Pacific war, and accompanied the convoy of 700 ships which were heading for Leyte.

The attack came at dawn and after the first forces had landed, he embarked for the shore on a landing craft, got out into the water, and waded ashore, followed by Sergio Osmena, who was now the President of the Philippines after Quezon had died, in August, much to MacArthur's deep regret. In a downpour of rain MacArthur manned a microphone to broadcast his message to the Philippine people. He said, 'People of the Philippines: I have returned. By the grace of Almighty God, our forces stand again on Philippine soil – soil consecrated by the blood of our two peoples.' It was a moment that MacArthur had long anticipated. He went on to say that Sergio Osmena was by his side and that the government of the Philippines was now 'firmly re-established on Philippine soil' He urged all Filipinos to 'rally to me. Let the indomitable spirit of Bataan and Corregidor lead on . . . In the name of your sacred dead, strike! Let no heart be faint. Let every arm be steeled. The guidance of Divine God points the way. Follow in His Name to the Holy Grail of righteous victory.' No matter what one may think of such prose today, MacArthur's words had an overwhelming impact on the Filipinos. MacArthur urged Roosevelt, in a note which he scribbled out on the beach, to grant the Philippines independence straightaway after the successful liberation campaign and asked Roosevelt to attend the ceremony in person. He wrote the President that 'such a step will electrify the world and redound immeasurably to the credit and honor of the United States for a thousand years.'

The Japanese were unimpressed by MacArthur's words or by the achievements of his landing force. On the 17th they became aware that the Americans were about to land on Leyte and threw a huge fleet into the battle. Had it not been for Admiral Kurita hesitating to press forward after his ships had sunk four ships of Admiral Kincaid's Seventh Fleet because of the heavy air attacks mounted by Halsey, the Allies might have suffered a stunning setback. As it was the Japanese squadrons did not reach Leyte Gulf, and the attack was successful. MacArthur once more pointed out that lack of co-ordination between the navy and the army could have caused a major disaster for the Allies.

Each day MacArthur went ashore to supervise the operations and one story, told by Kenney, described how MacArthur walked around wearing his field marshal's cap and smoking his ever-present corncob pipe. One soldier looked up and nudged his comrade and said, 'hey, there's General MacArthur.' The other soldier never even bothered to look around and replied, 'Oh yeah? And I suppose he's got Eleanor Roosevelt along with him.' MacArthur made certain that a plan to try disloyal Filipinos who were captured as traitors was scotched, and continued to supervise the take-over of Leyte, supported by Roosevelt. There were many impious comments put forward by some members of the forces who accompanied MacArthur to the Philippines. It was patently obvious that MacArthur was wringing the last ounce of public sentiment out of his return. Many claimed that MacArthur was trying to take all the credit, striding ashore to the Philippine beach while film cameras furiously clicked away. It was even mentioned that MacArthur could only have topped his performance by walking on the water to shore rather than through it. Despite his theatrical and quite typical performance, who can doubt that after the long struggles in New Guinea and through the islands MacArthur did not deserve his moment of melodrama? He had saved untold lives by finally agreeing to bypass Mindanao in favor of Leyte, and his strategy had paid off now that he had sufficient supplies to man his operations. His advice to Roosevelt was good; the United States would have stunned world public opinion had independence been granted soon after the victory. But, although there is a chance that Roosevelt, who loved amateur theatricals as much as MacArthur, might have done it, his death intervened. And the fight to recapture the Philippines was far from over.

By early December slow progress was being made. A landing on the west coast of Leyte went off without the loss of a single life, but the Japanese under General Yamashita were not prepared to give up the island or the Philippines themselves without a dogged fight. The airfields at Dulag and Tacloban were attacked, but the Japanese were faced with eight divisions, by far the largest force they had yet faced in the Pacific war. On 18th December, MacArthur was promoted to the rank of General of the Army, a new rank equivalent to that of field marshal. Eisenhower, Arnold and Marshall also received it at almost the same time. A story, perhaps apocryphal, is told of how this title evolved. Initially the title of field marshal was conceived, but since the first appointment was to go to George C Marshall, Marshall suggested that the title of Field Marshal Marshall might be slightly ludicrous, and the substitute General of the Army was proposed and accepted.

The mopping-up operation on Leyte, taken over from the Sixth Army by the Eighth Army on 26th December, proved to be far more serious than had been originally conceived. Although only about sixty to seventy thousand troops were engaged on the Japanese side, the Allies had put more than a quarter of a million men in the field. The Japanese lost an estimated 48,000 of their number, while only about 3,500 Allied lives were lost. Although MacArthur praised these troops vociferously – and with good reason, their ability to fight in the tropics, particularly in what might be described as jungle – the Americans tended to bog down. The Americans could put troops ashore in hostile territory and maintain supplies to them better than almost any other nation in the world, but a mechanized army finds itself more at home in the territory of another mechanized state like, say, Germany. When faced with alien territory, they tended to depend on heavy aerial bombardment and let the big guns do their work for them. This resulted in a slow progress but with comparatively little loss of life The American Army, composed largely of conscripts, unlike the marines or navy, lacked the *elan* that characterized many Continental armies, and certainly the Japanese Army. Their officers had to make up for this lack of *esprit de corps* through

The Leyte invasion fleet in the Admiralties before its departure

firepower and greatly superior numbers.

MacArthur was determined to land on Luzon as soon as possible, but was still meeting with opposition from Washington in the person of Admiral King. King still felt that Luzon should be bypassed in favor of Japan itself. Halsey, on the other hand, favored bypassing Formosa in favor of Luzon. Nimitz, at least until late September, favored attacking Formosa rather than Luzon. Almost without exception the ranking Army and Navy leaders in the Pacific were opposed to the seizure of Formosa; MacArthur had argued that a landing on Formosa would be very tricky and if, as Nimitz proposed, this operation would be followed by a landing at Amoy on the Chinese mainland, the Allies would be bogged down on the continent of China in much the same way as the Japanese had been since 1937. Although a Chinese invasion might have been supported by Clair Chennault's Tenth Air Force in Chungking, this would

have been peripheral, at best. By mid-September Leahy, Marshall and even the senior naval commanders all favored MacArthur's plan rather than Nimitz's; only King remained adamant. MacArthur had told the Joint Chiefs that he would be able to attack Luzon on 20th December, and on 3rd October MacArthur received a directive to attack on that date. Nimitz, meanwhile, was told to attack Iwo Jima in January, 1945 and Okinawa in March. The Joint Chiefs had decided, after all, to attack in the direction of Japan, their enemy, rather than China, their ally. MacArthur was relieved. He would not be cheated out of taking the whole of the Philippine archipelago, rather than just bits of it, as he once had feared.

MacArthur decided to land at Lingayen Gulf as the Japanese had done three years before. He also assumed that the Japanese would fight to the end, defending the Cagayan River and the Sierra Madre Mountains at the north of Luzon which MacArthur had

virtually left undefended in late 1941. His eventual plan was to take a weakly defended Mindoro on 5th December and make his landing on Luzon on the 20th, but the heavy fighting on Leyte delayed the operations to 15th December and 9th January respectively. Two regiments went ashore unopposed on Mindoro on the 15th and air strips were soon put in operation, but damage was done by Kamikaze raids as well as night air attacks. By the time the Luzon invasion was to take place, however, there were three fighter and two medium bomber groups based on Mindoro. At the same time Filipino guerrillas were strengthening their operations on Luzon, and they had provided intelligence for the whole of the Philippine exercise thus far. On the basis of this information MacArthur strengthened his invasion force for Luzon. The plan was to invade at Lingayen Gulf, then push across two flanks so as to secure both banks of the Agno River, and then thrust southward toward Manila. Halsey and the

The invasion of Leyte, 20th October 1944. *Above: USS Pennsylvania* fires on Japanese positions. *Right:* MacArthur and Sutherland offshore

Third Fleet would cover the invasion within range of both Formosa and Luzon. Kamikazes attacked the mine sweepers incessantly and two battleships and three cruisers were damaged by these suicide planes. But the Third Fleet arrived off Luzon on 3rd January, and MacArthur boarded the cruiser *Boise*. Submarines and Kamikazes continued their assaults and eleven more vessels were damaged. Several more ships were seriously damaged by these attacks in the days before the invasion but they had already run out of steam. Much of the Japanese air power had been destroyed in earlier raids and Kamikaze attacks, and Yamashita knew, just as MacArthur knew little more than three years before, that the loss of air superiority before an invasion took place spelled the success of the invasion. Yamashita planned to make his last stand in the northern mountains as MacArthur had done at Bataan.

The landing on 9th January found MacArthur wading ashore after his troops as President Osmena announced on the radio to his people that MacArthur himself was on Luzon. There was little Japanese opposition to the landings. but the retreat was slow and tedious, with heavy loss of life on both sides. The fighting around Clark Field, the major air base in the islands, was especially fierce, and MacArthur followed his troops toward Manila. MacArthur was awarded his third Distinguished Service Cross. For MacArthur this was a moment of genuine emotion. The Philippines were his country as much as the United States. His father had served there at the climax of his career and MacArthur himself had spent much of his life in service there. It was on the Philippines that he had suffered his worst defeat, and he was worshipped by the Filipinos. General Kenney dropped in one evening to report to him as the campaign progressed. MacArthur told him that he couldn't eat because of fatigue. The next morning before daybreak Kenney asked the orderly to say good-bye to MacArthur because he was leaving early. The officer told him that MacArthur left for the front over two hours before. Kenney is reported to have said, 'The guy must be nuts. If he works overtime, he'll lose his union card.' MacArthur's enthusiasm was only matched by the response of the Filipinos. The guerrillas sprang into action upon hearing of the landings in Luzon and made life increasingly difficult for the retreating Japanese.

As the Americans advanced MacArthur made his way to the concentration camps where belligerents and civilians alike who were left in the islands were taken for the duration

of the war by the Japanese. He was greeted by ragged, half-starved GIs at the Santo Tomas camp who wept and raced to him in the hopes of catching his hand. They wept at the sight of him. MacArthur was moved to near-speechlessness. The Americans entered Manila on 3rd February, almost four weeks after their landing, half as fast as the Japanese when they took the city in 1942. The enemy fought on sporadically for two more weeks before the city was firmly in American hands. In Manila, as elsewhere, Filipinos pressed round him, trying to touch him or kiss his hand and regale him with tears and thanks. His triumph was overwhelming. MacArthur was with his men and went to his penthouse atop the Manila Hotel where he had made his headquarters before the war. He had heard that everything was intact, untouched. As he approached the hotel, the Japanese set fire to it. He watched as his library of military history and the personal belongings of

Above: Leyte. After the preliminary bombardment, Marines move in aboard assault boats. *Right:* Marines climb inland off the beach

a lifetime, which had withstood the whole war, went up in flames.

By the end of January XIV Corps had secured Clark Field and were on the road leading to Bataan. On the 29th XI Corps, led by Major-General Charles P Hall, landed three regiments at the head of Subic Bay, the major naval base on Luzon. This operation would seal off the Bataan Peninsula while at the same time preventing the Japanese from landing any troops from Formosa to surprise the Americans in Lingayen Gulf. To secure the southern approaches to Manila, MacArthur sent Eichelberger to land one parachute regiment south of the city, and when the drop took place on 3rd February, it was unopposed. Meanwhile, the fight to eradicate the last remnants of Japanese resistance in Manila continued. Eventually the remaining opposition was trapped in the Intramuros, the old walled city section of Manila. After over a week of heavy artillery bombardment the infantry moved in on 23rd February, but the last die-hards did not capitulate until 3rd March. Heavy casualties were inflicted on both sides before the smoke cleared. MacArthur insisted that no delay should prevent the re-establishment of the powers of the Philippine Government even while the fighting for Manila continued. Although the city was rapidly being reduced to a smoldering ruin and the centuries-old Intramuros levelled, MacArthur restored constitutional government to the Philippines at a ceremony at the Malacanan Palace, sometimes known as the Philippine White House. The ceremony, held on 27th February, was a solemn one. MacArthur later described his trip to the Palace through the once-tree-lined streets past the

rubble and the unburied dead. When he finally arrived at the Malacanan, he found it untouched, with its stained glass windows, crystal chandeliers and tapestries all in place. In the presence of President Osmena, his senior commanders, and Osmena's cabinet he thought of all the memories he had of Manila, where he had courted his second wife, where his son had been born, where his father had served, and all the struggles and hopes that he had lived with in the Philippine capital. As he spoke to a hushed audience he recounted how his forces had fought back to regain Manila and the Philippines at such an exhorbitant cost. His voice broke and he was unable to go on as emotion overcame him.

MacArthur had insisted that the same degree of independence as formerly should be restored to the Philippine Government pending a final decision from Washington. It was

MacArthur wades ashore at Leyte with Osmena (left) and Sutherland

expected that full independence would be granted very soon, although it was not done until 4th July 1946. Meanwhile XI Corps had cleared Bataan, an operation which MacArthur personally supervised. Under heavy bombardment for weeks, the fortress island of Corregidor fell to the Americans, after having been defended almost to the last man by 5,000 Japanese troops. Most of them died on the island; only twenty-six were taken prisoner. MacArthur visited the island on 2nd March in four PT boats, the same number which left with his party when he embarked for Australia in 1942. Many of the same men who were with him that day returned with him to Corregidor to inspect the old headquarters. He raised the American flag atop the old flagpole.

By this time all of the main strategic objectives on Luzon had been taken. Although there were still Japanese

forces, the task remained to wipe out Yamashita's troops still in the northern highlands of Luzon. MacArthur was determined to eradicate every semblance of Japanese power in the Philippines, and even hoped to do the same in the Dutch East Indies, which he wanted to clear. Washington rejected this last proposal, and in so doing permitted Sukarno's Indonesian independence movement to seize power after the capitulation of Japan, since, aside from Dutch New Guinea, there were no Allied troops occupying the Dutch East Indies when Japan finally fell. By April the sea route through the Visayas was cleared, and by the end of June the Japanese only held about a twenty-five mile square area. near the summer capital of Baguio. The Americans lost 8,500 lives in securing Luzon and upon capitulation there were still some 50,000 Japanese troops who had held out, almost 40,000 of these being with Yamashita's group. Baguio fell on

26th April, but the Japanese retreated to a small pocket north-east of the city. During this same period Iwo Jima had been taken with a heavy loss of American lives. The Japanese defense of the Philippines had been admirable. They engaged tens of thousands of American troops, just as the Japanese had stalled American naval and air forces at Iwo Jima, and by late spring, 1945, after Germany had capitulated, the Allies were still far from achieving complete victory over Japan. It was widely felt that the war in the Pacific would last quite a long time yet, and that Japan would have to be fought over for a year to a year and a half before their spirit would be broken. The Kamikaze missions, which grew in ferocity during the first months of 1945, convinced MacArthur and most other American military leaders that Japan would not go down without a long and arduous fight on the four main islands themselves after the Ryukyus were occupied.

On the day MacArthur's troops entered Manila a conference took place on the other side of the world which was to influence the course of the war in the Pacific. Yalta, the penultimate Allied conference, attended by Roosevelt, Churchill and Stalin, decided that Russia would enter the war in the Pacific two to three months after the capitulation of Germany. Russia was promised southern Sakhalin, Port Arthur and Dairen in southern Manchuria, which they had lost to Japan in 1905 as well as an occupation zone in Korea, their old sphere of influence, and the Kurile Islands. Roosevelt's reasoning was based on reports that he had received from the Far East, including reports sent by MacArthur. Japan would be a hard nut to crack, and with their reputedly large reserve force still untested in the Kwantung Peninsula, the Allies felt that Russian help would bring the war to a speedier conclusion. Although it is now known that the Kwantung Army had been greatly reduced and was not nearly the formidable weapon it was thought to be, it was not unreasonable to ask Russia at that time to help win the war in the Pacific, despite the fact that this decision was to come under heavy criticism later, with MacArthur one of the chief critics. The fight on Okinawa, which began on 1st April, did not lead the Americans and their allies to change their point of view, as the Japanese fought bitterly and bravely against increasingly more powerful opposition.

On 1st May, MacArthur's Australians opened the first phase of what was to be a longterm plan to recapture the Dutch East Indies. Roosevelt had not wanted MacArthur to engage American troops in these operations and MacArthur, distrustful of the British, was unhappy about the prospect of sending British forces to clear the Indies, as he felt that if they took the the territory, it would be difficult to dislodge them. Although the problems of Raffles in Java during and after the Napoleonic Wars were an example of

Above: The warrior returns. MacArthur broadcasts to the Philippine people
Below: MacArthur proclaims the liberation of the Philippines

what could have happened, it is doubtful whether MacArthur's fears had any real basis. The British had an alliance with the Netherlands and had promised them – or at least Churchill had done – that the Indies would be restored to Holland after the war.

Roosevelt had died on 12th April, and was replaced by Harry S Truman, former US Senator from Missouri and Vice-President since January 1945. Although MacArthur had a grudging respect for his onetime nemesis, Roosevelt, he knew little about Truman and felt that he knew a good deal more about the situation in the Far East than his new commander-in-chief. In any event, MacArthur felt that if Australian (they were near enough to be British in his eyes) forces moved into the Dutch East Indies under his own command, they could be prevented from repeating Raffles' errors in trying to remain in possession of the archipelago. They were assigned to seize Tarakan near eastern Borneo as the first step in this operation. MacArthur refused to use British troops under Mountbatten's command for the recapture of the Indies for another reason: they would be cutting into what MacArthur felt was his territory and reap the fruits of victory which they had done so little to merit, at least with respect to the Indies. Their record in Burma speaks for itself. Furthermore, the oil of Borneo could be used to supply MacArthur's own campaigns.

General Sir Thomas Blamey of the Australian Army strongly objected to MacArthur's implication that the Australians were not to be trusted. He wanted to have effective control over his own forces and complained bitterly to the Australian Defence Department. When Blamey met MacArthur they compromised by agreeing that although the Australian I Corps would operate under Blamey's effective control, with the 'administrative functions' performed by Blamey's advance HQ at Morotai, the unit would remain under MacArthur's general command. Blamey had no intention of withdrawing Australian troops from Australian New Guinea – there were still some Japanese soldiers left withering on the vine behind Allied lines who were maintaining a rear guard action – for combat in the Dutch East Indies until the last remnants of Japanese resistance were rooted out. In this respect Blamey, quite naturally, looked upon Australian New Guinea in much the same way as MacArthur viewed the Philippines. It was a matter of his country's honor, its self-respect.

Plans for Borneo were finally sorted out by the Combined Chiefs of Staff. The plans were revised to assure that Tarakan would be taken in May, Brunei Bay in June and Balikpapan in July. The British, contrary to what MacArthur thought about them, were not really anxious that action be taken against Borneo. Japan, after all, was the principal objective and Borneo was in the opposite direction from Japan with the bulk of Allied strength now in the Philippines. The British point of view did not prevail, and it seems ironic that in the effort (ostensibly) to prevent British imperialist interests from re-asserting themselves in Southeast Asia, MacArthur made every effort to replace their imperial designs by American ones, despite all that MacArthur has said to the contrary.

MacArthur ruefully pointed out in his memoirs that the restoration of Dutch rule to the Indies would have provided a more orderly administration of the area, and that the plans he harbored for a complete reconquest of the Indies were foiled by mal-administration from Washington, the result of which was the 'chaos' which ensued after the Japanese capitulation. This chaos, one is to assume, took the form of the establishment of the Indonesian government under Sukarno and their declaration of independence on 17th

August, 1945. That there was political and military strife in Indonesia after the end of the war cannot be doubted. But MacArthur can hardly claim to be an anti-imperialist when he sought so hard to re-establish Dutch, in favor of British, imperial interests in Southeast Asia after the war.

An Australian brigade group landed on Tarakan on 1st May. Soon afterwards Germany, capitulated and the Australian government, at Blamey's request, asked MacArthur if he could reconsider his plan to continue to Balikpapan rather than sending Australian forces along with the Americans against Japan. The Australian people were as anxious as the other allies to end the war in the Pacific as soon as possible now that the fighting in Europe was over. MacArthur insisted that the operation in Borneo be continued and that the Australians continue to make their way toward Balikpapan, and they agreed despite their misgivings. MacArthur even went so far as to go ashore with the Australian forces when they secured Brunei Bay in June, and did the same thing at Balikpapan on 1st July when an amphibious attack was launched there involving 33,000 troops. It was to be the last operation of MacArthur's Southwest Pacific Command and it was done expertly, as usual.

Within three weeks it was all over except for some mopping-up activity. By July 1945 the fight on Luzon was still not over. It was the largest land campaign of the Pacific war and involved fifteen American divisions as well as substantial numbers of Philippine troops, more than the Allies had in Sicily, or Burma, or Okinawa. MacArthur's insistence that the last remnants of Japanese opposition be eradicated on the Philippines before committing his troops to the invasion of Japan did not shorten the war in the Pacific. His plans, had they been carried out, to recapture the Dutch East Indies would not have made the war any shorter either. His original scheme of island hopping and bypassing the Japanese whenever possible, which was so successful on New Guinea and after, should have been continued, but MacArthur's conception of his own honor and his nation's stood in the way. However, MacArthur was still under the impression that the war in the Pacific was far from over, and had told President Truman that he would need at least another year, probably more, to defeat Japan on her own ground.

It was on the basis of this and other similar arguments that Truman made the decision which was to end the war so dramatically – the dropping of the atomic bomb on Hiroshima – a decision about which MacArthur had no prior knowledge.

The seizure of Okinawa made the bombing and subsequent invasion of Japan possible by July 1945. The fire raids on Japanese cities, particularly Tokyo, advocated by Major-General Curtis LeMay, were having a devastating effect on the civilian population, but the Japanese were thoroughly prepared to fight to the bitter end.

MacArthur and Nimitz had already made preliminary plans for the invasion of the home islands, which was to take place on Kyushu, Japan's southern-most island, and was to be of unparalleled magnitude. Although Nimitz and MacArthur would cooperate, the divided command was to be sustained even at this terminal stage. The Allies expected a force of approximately two million men to greet them in Japan itself, and it was thought that an initial landing force of about ten divisions with a reserve of three more would be required. A landing near Tokyo was to follow, and fourteen more divisions plus about eleven more in reserve would be required. On 17th July the final wartime conference began at Potsdam, outside occupied Berlin, in which Truman, Stalin and Churchill met to discuss the Allied settlement in Europe as well as the concluding stages of the war against Japan. Churchill was soon replaced by

The clearing-up operation on Leyte dragged on for several months. *Above:* Marines cross a water tank trap. *Below:* A young prisoner

Above: The American armada in Lingayen Gulf, Luzon, January 1945. Heavy AA fire is being maintained on Japanese planes. *Below:* MacArthur wading ashore in Luzon

Clement Attlee, whose Labour Party was elected to office at the British general elections which took place while the conference was in session.

As the conference began Truman was informed of the successful atomic tests then under way in New Mexico, and soon after authorized the dropping of this weapon on Japan in an attempt to avoid the necessity of an Allied invasion which was sure to cost tens of thousands of American lives. The Japanese were offered the choice of facing the new weapon, described to them in the broadest terms, or capitulating at once. Japan characteristically refused to accept defeat on the basis of threats and refused to negotiate a surrender which the Allies had made clear years before would be unconditional. On 6th August, 1945 a single American airplane, the *Enola Gay*, dropped the most devastating weapon yet known to man on the city of Hiroshima and uniformly levelled the city.

President Truman announced this event to the American people some hours later, telling his countrymen that the atomic bomb had more power than twenty thousand tons of TNT. He went on to point out that the Americans were determined to continue these attacks in order to 'completely destroy Japan's power to make war.' On 8th August Russia, ironically keeping to their word given at the Yalta Conference that they would enter the war two or three months after the capitulation of Germany, attacked Japanese forces in Manchukuo, Japanese-controlled Manchuria, three months to the day after the war in Europe ended. The Soviet Union formally declared war against Japan. The Japanese government refused to accept defeat even after the first bomb was dropped, so on the following day, 9th August, a second atomic bomb was dropped on Nagasaki. By 10th August Japan had had enough. On 12th August Truman ordered his air force to cease its incessant bombing raids on Japan. On 15th August Japan surrendered.

Although MacArthur did not participate in the negotiations which led to the capitulation, on the day Japan surrendered MacArthur was appointed Supreme Commander Allied Powers, which placed him in charge of organizing the ceremonies of surrender as well as the occupation and re-organization of postwar Japan. He directed the Imperial government to send a delegation to Manila to receive their instructions concerning the surrender ceremonies. Sutherland handled most of the talks with the Japanese, who were extremely co-operative except for one point: they protested against the preparations at Atsugi airfield near Yokohama, which they felt could not be made ready in time for MacArthur's arrival. Propellers on all Japanese aircraft were ordered to be removed before he arrived, armed troops were to be withdrawn from the Tokyo area, and vehicles were to be provided for the use of the Allies. MacArthur would make his headquarters in the New Grand Hotel in Yokohama. Many of MacArthur's advisers advised him not to go to Atsugi, which had been used by Kamikaze pilots who denounced the surrender in no uncertain terms, even dropping leaflets to the Japanese people and threatening to bomb the battleship *Missouri* on which the formal surrender ceremonies would take place.

There was a great deal of uncertainty about how the Japanese would treat their conqueror, inasmuch as there were still twenty-two Japanese divisions, comprising over 300,000 men, on the Kanto Plain near Tokyo and Yokohama. But the broadcast of the Emperor, an unprecedented act, tended to calm most of the population. Repeating the words of his predecessor, the Emperor Meiji, who had remarked that Japan had to 'accept the unacceptable, endure the unendurable' when the Far Eastern Triplice had thwarted Japan's attempts to take over Port Arthur, Dairen and the Kwantung Peninsula

after the Sino-Japanese War in 1895, the Showa Emperor, Hirohito, told his stunned nation that 'as he [Meiji] endured the unendurable, so shall I, and so must you.' Hirohito waited in the Imperial Palace not knowing what his fate was to be. MacArthur was determined from the outset that the divinity of the Emperor should be destroyed, but he also had sufficient knowledge of the Japanese people to know that to eliminate the Emperor himself would be a serious error.

The Potsdam Declaration of a month before was to be the basis of Mac-Arthur's new position in Japan, and it was a broad enough brief to suit MacArthur's attitude. It stated that those who brought Japan to war should be eliminated 'for all time', that Japan should be occupied militarily, that stern justice should be meted out to 'war criminals', and that democratic government and the freedoms which usually accompany it should be established in Japan; the Allies would withdraw their

Above: Clark Field in Northern Luzon was taken only after heavy fighting
Right: MacArthur gives his blessing to Filipino guerrillas

occupation forces once this mission had been completed. On 29th August MacArthur received a summary of the US Initial Post-Surrender Policy for Japan which had been prepared by the State Department as well as the War and Navy Departments. This document gave MacArthur the authority to control Japan 'through Japanese governmental machinery and agencies, including the Emperor.' Therefore it has been accepted that the Emperor would remain on his throne, although the character of his régime would change radically. Mac-Arthur's initial conception that the Emperor should be retained as an instrument of peace was maintained by the American government, and MacArthur was to have free rein in Japan based on the broad proposals outlined in the document.

From 25th August on aircraft and a few infantry were landed in Japan under Eichelberger, and their fears that they would meet severe diehard opposition proved unfounded. The Emperor's speech had shattered the will of the Japanese people to continue their struggles. Veneration, far greater then mere respect, for the Emperor was so great that it was unthinkable for most Japanese to oppose what he had said was his will. The voice of the Emperor had never been heard in Japan; he had never made broadcasts as Roosevelt, de Gaulle and King George had done. His position in the Japanese social and governmental hierarchy could not be challenged. The war had been fought in his name. He was, more than any Western monarch had ever been in the heyday of absolute monarchy, the fountainhead of government and power. Therefore, when he surrendered publicly and accepted public humiliation at the end of the war, the vast majority of the people of Japan followed him. It was, indeed, only through him that any opposition to the Allied occupation which did exist could be suppressed. The Japanese, whose islands had never been occupied by an invader in all their long history, awaited their fate.

At the same time more than 350 ships of the American and British Pacific Fleets steamed toward Tokyo Bay. Even the locale of the surrender ceremonies was contested by interservice rivalry, which continued to the very end. The compromise was reached when it was agreed that MacArthur of the army would accept the surrender on Nimitz's flagship the *Missouri*, which also pleased Truman, whose home state was Missouri. A regiment of marines would be sent ashore while army troops landed at Atsugi. Furthermore, the army and navy would share in the initial occupa-

tion of Japan. The Eighth Army and
Third Fleet were responsible for
Honshu, the principal island of Japan,
from Kobe eastward. The Sixth Army
and Fifth Fleet were to occupy western Honshu, Kyushu and Shikoku, the
North Pacific Fleet was to occupy
Hokkaido, and the Seventh Fleet and
XXIV Corps were to occupy Korea
south of the 38th Parallel. Russia was
to occupy (and was rapidly occupying)
Manchuria and Korea north of the
38th Parallel. Ships of the Third Fleet
entered Tokyo Bay on the 28th and
troops were landed at Yokusaka on
the 30th.

Early in the morning of the 30th
MacArthur boarded his aircraft
Bataan for the seven-hour flight to
Tokyo. MacArthur made notes on the
plane which were to become the
broad outlines for his policy as
military governor for the next six
years. At 2pm the *Bataan* circled
Atsugi airfield and landed, giving
MacArthur a view of Mount Fujiyama
as the aircraft turned. MacArthur

Above: MacArthur, with his trademark,
in Manila. *Right:* Troops prepare to
attack Intramuros, the walled city in
Manila

quietly got out of the plane, dressed
in an open-necked shirt and puffing
on his corncob pipe. Despite the fact
that there was great apprehension
that at the last minute diehard
Japanese would storm the small
military contingent which was there
to greet him, MacArthur appeared
calm and resolute. General Eichelberger greeted him and as they shook
hands MacArthur said: 'Bob, from
Melbourne to Tokyo is a long way,
but this seems to be the end of the
road.' Along the road to Yokohama a
long line of Japanese soldiers guarded
the route, giving MacArthur the
same respect that they paid the
Emperor; their backs were turned as
his cortège passed. Yokohama seemed
like a ghost town when MacArthur
arrived. Shop windows were boarded
up, blinds were drawn and the side-

Above: Corregidor is retaken. MacArthur is present as the American flag is raised once more. *Below:* Marines attack at Iwo Jima

The Big·Three at the Yalta Conference, February 1945

walks seemed deserted. He went to the New Grand Hotel, where he planned to stay until he made his formal entry into Tokyo. There was no incident whatever, and the hotel management treated him with servile deference. After checking into his suite, MacArthur simply repaired to the dining room where he devoured a steak dinner.

As prisoners from POW camps were being released MacArthur insisted that Generals Wainwright and Percival be brought to Japan to attend the ceremonies on the *Missouri*. On the night of the 31st they arrived at MacArthur's hotel, haggard, drawn and emaciated from their years in prison camp. MacArthur was just sitting down to dinner when he heard that they had arrived. As MacArthur rose to greet them in the lobby, the doors of the dining room swung open and there was Wainwright. MacArthur later reported that 'his uniform hung in folds on his fleshless form. He walked with difficulty and with the help of a cane. His eyes were sunken and there were pits in his cheeks.' MacArthur embraced his colleague, who said he felt that he had disgraced MacArthur and his nation by capitulating at Corregidor. Mac-

Arthur was shocked by this remark and said, 'your old corps is yours when you want it.' Wainwright was greatly relieved and MacArthur was moved beyond words.

The ceremony on the *Missouri* took place on 2nd September, 1945. The Foreign Minister of Japan, Shigemitsu, accepted the onerous duty of signing the surrender documents on behalf of the Emperor, and the Emperor had to personally persuade the second delegate, General Umezu, to agree to attend. The destroyers carrying the party to the *Missouri* arrived on that perfect day with blue skies and the American flag, the one used by Commodore Perry at Tokyo Bay almost a hundred years before, waving proudly in the breeze. Umezu was dressed in the olive drab of a general officer, with shiny cavalry boots and a ceremonial sword at his side. Mamoru Shigemitsu was dressed in a formal top hat, morning coat and striped trousers. Admiral 'Bull' Halsey, whose own ship was being used, was the host and greeted the Japanese delegation. There were row upon row of glittering uniforms of the representatives of all the Allied powers to greet the Japanese as well. The ship was jam-

Okinawa, April 1945. A flamethrower ready, Marines advance on the Japanese

med with military personnel, cameramen and reporters. MacArthur, in contrast with everyone, was wearing a simple uniform with his shirt open at the neck, without decorations, his ubiquitous cap atop his head. Some Japanese thought his unformal attire to have been a studied insult. More likely it was MacArthur's taste for the theatrical, so that he could stand out against all the sparkle and pomp of the uniforms which surrounded him.

At precisely nine o'clock MacArthur strode out on deck and read from a bit of white paper that he held in his hand, standing behind a table which faced the Japanese. His speech was short. He said that the representatives of the Allied powers had come to restore peace with Japan. He added that it was not their purpose to meet 'in a spirit of distrust, malice or hatred. But rather it is for

us, both victors and vanquished, to rise to that higher dignity which alone befits the sacred purposes we are about to serve . . . It is my earnest hope and indeed the hope of all mankind that from this solemn occasion a better world shall emerge out of the blood and carnage of the past – a world founded upon faith and understanding – a world dedicated to the dignity of man and the fulfillment of his most cherished wish – for freedom, tolerance and justice.' After the speech was over the Japanese delegates moved to the table to sign the surrender documents. At eight minutes past nine MacArthur put his name to the surrender, followed by representatives of the Allied powers. Shigemitsu nervously signed the document, slumping forward on the table, and Sutherland showed him where to sign. Wainwright and Nimitz were among those who signed for the United States. When the representatives of the other nations (China, the United Kingdom, the Soviet Union,

Australia, Canada, France, the Netherlands and New Zealand) had signed, MacArthur announced: 'Let us pray that peace be now restored to the world and that God will preserve it always. These proceedings' are closed.' A deafening roar from over a thousand planes which flew past overhead brought the historic ceremonies to a close. Soon afterwards MacArthur broadcast a message to the American people. The Second World War at last was over.

MacArthur established his headquarters in Tokyo on 8th September and his long reign as Supreme Commander Allied Powers, *de facto* ruler of Japan, had begun. The story of MacArthur's career in Japan and Korea is one which must be told elsewhere, but in 1945 MacArthur had reached the pinnacle of a long and honored career. He was a great soldier. His strong and dominating character was strengthened by his experiences in the First World War, where he displayed courage and leadership matched by very few indeed. But a warrior in peacetime undergoes subtle changes of character. The years between the wars were frustrating ones for MacArthur, even though the posts which he held were served with distinction. MacArthur craved action and he also recognized the need for the United States to wake up from its postwar lethargy and irresponsibility to the realities which the 1930s presented - a renascent Germany, an aggressive Italy and an increasingly belligerent Japan. Deprived of the funds necessary to build up the defenses in the Philippines, his petulant attitude prevented him from doing more than what was done. He blamed Washington for his failings, and up until the time of his second marriage, his pride got the better of his judgement. The court-like atmosphere in Manila which appealed to his fantasies of grandeur and melodrama caused a deterioration in his character that was to have shattering consequences when the war broke out. Regardless of what he may have said to the contrary, MacArthur had not done an adequate job in preparing the Philippines for the attack, and the fault cannot be laid at the feet of Washington exclusively. His retreat to Bataan and Corregidor was badly handled, and the poor morale among his beleaguered troops there was largely his own fault.

It is difficult to guess what another man's thoughts are, and memoirs often serve as a disguise rather than a mirror to them. But one can hazard an assumption that in the first bleak months in Australia, MacArthur knew that he had failed. It was not so much out of revenge against Japan but as a sop to his own bad conscience that MacArthur pressed for an early return to the Philippines and, once there, insisted on driving every single Japanese soldier from the islands rather than concentrating on a major push towards Japan. But his conduct of the New Guinea campaign, his reconquest of the Philippines were brilliantly executed. Although detractors of MacArthur have argued that it was Halsey as much as the Joint Chiefs who engineered these successful operations, the fact remains that MacArthur was the general in charge, and as such, did an excellent job. He saved his reputation and made a new and better one as a conquering general.

This rehabilitation of his scarred reputation marked a real renascence in his own character as well. He was pompous, blustery, imperious and egotistical - all of these things - but he did a fine job and he knew it. So did Roosevelt and Marshall, who, vexed by his querulousness in 1942 and 1943, recognized his military abilities and gave him what he needed when they could. On the other hand, his political acumen left a lot to be desired. His understanding of American politics was naive, not to put too fine a point on it. Although he cannot be blamed for the way he handled the Bonus Marchers, since he was acting

Above left: The Potsdam conference, July 1945. Truman greets Atlee and Bevin, the new rulers of Britain. *Below left:* MacArthur with Wainright (right) and Percival after their release. *Above:* The historic meeting of MacArthur and Emperor Hirohito

under the strict instructions of his superiors, he seemed to overestimate the influence of sinister and subversive forces among the Marchers. He was a man of the extreme right in the political spectrum, but as long as he stuck to military problems, this really didn't seem to matter. All generals have an authoritarian streak; otherwise they wouldn't be generals. MacArthur carried this authoritarian image to extremes. When first in Australia he tended to blame others for his short-comings, and did not understand or accept the decision to defeat Hitler first rather than Japan. His nagging of Washington, however, resulted in getting more men and supplies than he otherwise would have received and he put them to good use.

He was not a waster of men; his casualty record was low, and if the use of heavy firepower was required to win the war in the Pacific without an undue loss of life, then one can hardly criticize him for demanding more armaments, planes and ships. It was when his ego got the better of him, in the Philippine campaign, where he committed too many men to the reconquest of the archipelago when he should have concentrated on the conquest of Japan. But one has to return to his worst weakness – his belief in his own infallibility which was nurtured by a sycophantic staff which he kept around him. He made military mistakes, as all generals do, but he brooked no criticism. It was only when he ventured to self-criticize, when in Australia, that he was able to pull himself up by his own boot-

157

The Japanese surrender to MacArthur on *USS Missouri* in Tokyo Bay, 31st August 1945

straps and get down to the serious business of winning the war.

His taste for the melodramatic, one of his worst faults, actually aided him and his conduct of the Pacific war. His grandiose statements to the press appealed to the American people and helped build morale in the United States when the going was tough in the first months after America entered the war. Many generals would have been fired after a debacle such as MacArthur presided over in Bataan and Corregidor. MacArthur's prose saved his career. He was too popular to be dismissed, and through his own personal comeback, many Americans could live vicariously through his triumphs. His men may have resented his comments at times; but this resentment evolved into an attitude of grudging admiration for a general who would go ashore with his troops on many occasions, although he was a man in his sixties, even though they knew he did it as much to acquire public recognition for his own heroism as to build morale among his troops.

But it was one thing for MacArthur to attack his Commander-in-Chief on military grounds; it is the duty of any officer to question the wisdom of his political masters when it comes to waging war. But it is quite another thing to attack his President or Joint Chiefs of Staff on political grounds, where soldiers often are at their most vulnerable. With all his weaknesses, this was MacArthur's worst, and it was to be painfully exposed in his postwar career which was marked by brilliance as Japan's new *shogun* as well as hesitancy and political ignorance as commander of the United Nations forces in Korea. But that is another story. It cannot erase his greatest qualities: his patriotism, his personal courage, his excellence, after all is said and done, as a military commander.

159

Bibliography

MacArthur as Military Commander by Gavin Long (Batsford, London)
Reminiscences by Douglas MacArthur (McGraw Hill, New York)
MacArthur 1941-1951 by C A Willoughby and J Chamberlain (Heinemann, London)
Front-Line General: Douglas MacArthur by Jules Archer (Bailey Bros, London. Julian Messner, New York)
But Not in Shame by John Toland (Panther Books, London. Signet Books, New York)
The Road to Pearl Harbor by Herbert Feis (Atheneum, New York)
Pearl Harbor: Warning and Decision by Roberta Wohlstetter (Oxford University Press, London. Stanford University Press, Stanford)
The United States and Japan by Edwin O Reischauer (Oxford University Press, London. Harvard University Press, Cambridge, Mass)
The Fall of Japan by William Craig (Weidenfeld & Nicholson, London. Dial Press, New York)
Hirohito: Emperor of Japan by Leonard Moseley (Weidenfeld & Nicholson, London)
Between War and Peace: The Potsdam Conference by Herbert Feis (Oxford University Press, London, Princeton University Press, Princeton)